NEW
BOOK

Celebrating
Interfaith Marriages

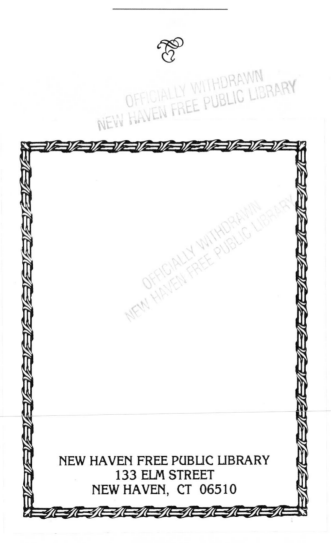

Celebrating Interfaith Marriages

CREATING YOUR

JEWISH/CHRISTIAN

CEREMONY

Rabbi Devon A. Lerner

PREFACE BY

Rev. Nicholas C. Ciccone, Jr., Ph.D.

AN OWL BOOK

HENRY HOLT AND COMPANY ♥ NEW YORK

Henry Holt and Company, Inc.
Publishers since 1866
115 West 18th Street
New York, New York 10011

Henry Holt® is a registered
trademark of Henry Holt and Company, Inc.

Published in Canada by Fitzhenry & Whiteside Ltd.,
195 Allstate Parkway, Markham, Ontario L3R 4T8.

Library of Congress Cataloging-in-Publication Data
Lerner, Devon A.
Celebrating interfaith marriages: creating your
Jewish/Christian ceremony / Devon A. Lerner.—1st ed.
p.   cm.
"An Owl book."
ISBN 0-8050-6083-9 (pbk.: alk. paper)
1. Interfaith marriage services.   2. Marriage—Religious aspects—Judaism.
3. Marriage—Religious aspects—Christianity.   4. Weddings—Planning.   I. Title.
HQ745.L455   1999
395.2'2—dc21   98-38274
                                                                    CIP

Henry Holt books are available for special promotions
and premiums. For details contact: Director, Special Markets.

First Edition 1999

Designed by Victoria Hartman

Printed in the United States of America
All first editions are printed on acid-free paper. ∞
1   3   5   7   9   10   8   6   4   2

To My Parents

Frances and Meyer Lerner

Contents

Part II ♥ Sample Ceremonies

Part III ♥ Menu of Passages
for Each Element of the Service

Part IV ♥ Wedding Readings

Appendix I ♥ Traditional Wedding Ceremonies

Appendix II ♥ Ketubot

Appendix III ♥ Hebrew Prayers with Their Transliterations and Translations

Acknowledgments

I owe a great deal of thanks to many people who have supported and encouraged me throughout the years of writing this book. To Caitlin Williams, my dearest friend, for her daily support and patience. To Jan Rabinowitch, whose gentle encouragement and laughter helped me begin and persevere, and to Rabbi Donald Pollock and Betsy Pollock, my colleagues, cheerleaders, and kindred spirits, whose humor, confidence, and feedback helped me complete this project.

A special note of thanks to my literary agent, Meredith Bernstein, who believed in this project from the start. I feel very fortunate to have her support and expertise. To Father Nicholas Ciccone, for his patient editing and instruction. To my editor, Amelia Sheldon, for her wonderful support and guidance throughout this process, and to both Amelia and Owl Books/Henry Holt and Company, Inc., for their enthusiasm about and commitment to this book.

And finally, and most importantly, to all of the dozens of couples who contributed their writing, resources, thoughts, and feelings. Their work forms the essence of this book.

Preface

꩜

Roman Catholic priests and pastors are ordained to serve our congregations during their entire lives, from birth to death. We are called to minister to the engaged, married couples, parents, developing families, hurting families, and to help couples and families in all areas of their relationships and faith.

Couples preparing for marriage are a high priority within the Church, because the health of a marriage affects a person's well-being, children, and relationships with families, school, and work. A healthy marriage builds the fabric of our society, our church, and faith.

Of particular concern to the Church are couples choosing to marry a non-Catholic partner. An interfaith marriage requires a great deal of understanding, work, and commitment on the part of the couple. This book provides a practical guide for an interfaith couple to begin the process of planning a healthy marriage and family life as well as a meaningful wedding ceremony.

An interfaith wedding ceremony is an important way for a couple to begin their married lives, reflecting the common values and beliefs we share. So often we confuse uniformity of practice with unity of belief. The Jewish and Catholic communities worship the one God that watches over us all.

This book will be an important resource for couples planning an interfaith marriage. I have found it a valuable resource in my own work with interfaith couples.

Rev. Nicholas C. Ciccone, Jr., Ph.D.

Introduction

Interfaith marriages are a fact of life. Today more than fifty percent of Jewish men and women are marrying non-Jewish, mostly Christian, partners. Even though hundreds, if not thousands, of these weddings occur each year, there are still few resources to help couples create a ceremony that honors the beliefs and feelings of both partners. I wrote this book to help meet this growing demand and need.

Much of the material in these pages comes from the hundreds of interfaith couples I have married. Their thoughts, their feelings, and, in many cases, their own words are contained in this book. My sincere thanks to all of them for their ingenuity and their generosity. Their gifts will help scores of others create their own personalized ceremonies.

The Intermarriage Controversy

While interfaith marriages are common, most rabbis refuse to officiate at interfaith weddings. Orthodox and Conservative rabbis refuse to participate because they believe Jewish law forbids their involvement. According to that law, a marriage between a Jew and a non-Jew is not considered valid. Many Reform, or liberal, rabbis refuse to participate because they believe interfaith marriages are hastening the assimilation of the Jewish community into our secular American society. Since most interfaith couples do not raise their children as Jews, Reform rabbis often see each interfaith marriage as one less Jewish family for the next generation. Less than three percent of the American population is Jewish, so each practicing Jewish family counts to those interested in keeping the community strong.

Those who do officiate argue that this hard-line approach alienates both the Jewish and non-Jewish partner. They feel it is better to bless, rather than reject, these couples. Then, the Jewish partner will feel affirmed in his/her identity, and the couple will be more inclined to raise their children as Jews.

While each rabbi must decide for him or herself whether or not to participate in interfaith weddings, Catholic priests are obligated by Church law to do everything in their power to promote healthy marriages, which includes the blessing of and participation in interfaith marriages. In spite of this stance, it is often difficult for couples to find a priest who will officiate because many priests personally oppose interfaith marriages. They believe that these marriages weaken the Catholic community in similar ways that some rabbis believe interfaith marriages weaken the Jewish community. But regardless of a priest's personal beliefs, he is directed by Church law to help interfaith couples with their wedding. If the local pastor refuses or is unable to participate, the Catholic party can call the bishop's office for assistance.

Protestant clergy usually feel less conflicted than rabbis and priests about participating in interfaith weddings. But it is important to understand that interfaith marriages are impacting every religious community in this country, and each community is struggling to find ways to meet this challenge while maintaining their beliefs and customs.

This trend of marriage among people of different faiths has generated many responses, some of which embrace and others of which alienate interfaith families.

The purpose of this book, however, is not to justify or debate any of these positions, but to provide resources for those who have chosen to marry someone of a different faith and who wish to exchange their vows in a ceremony that honors the beliefs and feelings of both partners.

The Contents

This book is divided into four parts. Part I includes some information about the emotional side of interfaith weddings, a detailed outline and description of the structure and content of interfaith ceremonies, a discussion of conflicts between Christian and Jewish customs, an explanation of details that can enhance any ceremony, a checklist of items to bring to the wedding, and a step-by-step guide to creating your own ceremony. Part II contains several sample interfaith ceremonies. Part III includes a menu of passages for each element of a service. Part IV contains a collection of biblical and modern poetry and prose. By using the information and material from each section, any couple can create their own interfaith ceremony.

About gender exclusive language: You will notice that some of the sample ceremonies and many of the biblical and secular readings contain gender exclusive language. The pronouns "he," "him," and "his" are used as generic terms referring to God or to both men and women. While I personally object to this style, I feel it is important, and in some cases legally necessary, not to alter the language of a couple's or author's work in order to make them gender inclusive. When you create your own ceremony, you can choose or change the words to suit your needs and tastes.

To gay and lesbian couples: If you are using this book to help you create your own commitment or marriage ceremony, simply replace references to the bride and groom with "partners," "life companions," or any other term that you like. Of course, planning for your ceremony and celebration is not as simple as substituting a few words in a service. You face many emotional issues that heterosexual couples do not, issues that are not addressed in these pages. Four books that do address your special needs and concerns are *Recognizing Ourselves: Ceremonies of Lesbian and Gay Commitment*, by Ellen Lewin; *Equal Rites: Lesbian and Gay Worship, Ceremonies and Celebrations*, edited by Kittredge Cherry and Zalmon Sherwood; *Lesbian and Gay Marriage: Private Commitments, Public Ceremonies*, edited by Suzanne Sherman; and *Ceremonies of the Heart*, edited by Becky Butler. The Internet is also another good source of information.

I hope that this book will enable you to design a ceremony that you will remember fondly for the rest of your life.

Celebrating
Interfaith Marriages

· PART I ·

Interfaith Weddings

On the Emotional Side

Creating your own ceremony can be fun and exciting. The process provides you as a couple with a unique opportunity to express your love in words that speak to your own hearts and souls. But the thought of creating such a ceremony scares many people. Few know where to begin, and many doubt their creative abilities. If you are feeling a bit uncertain, let me assure you that regardless of your background or level of religious education, you can craft a beautiful ceremony. All the information you need is in these pages. I will lead you step-by-step through this process, one that is easier than most imagine.

But before I begin talking about ceremonies, I want to address some of the emotional issues that often accompany wedding-day preparations.

Between You and Your Partner

When you announced your engagement, you were full of excitement and joy. Now, as you begin planning for your wedding day, you may feel a great deal of stress. This is normal. Planning any wedding, regardless of size, is stressful because of the endless number of details, including everything from choosing the color of your napkins, to deciding who will preside over your service, to managing the wishes and feelings of two different families. These details consume more time and energy than most couples anticipate, even when they have a wedding coordinator; so try to give yourselves enough space between your engagement and your wedding day to handle all of the arrangements. For most couples, this means starting the wedding planning at least a year in advance. Many popular wedding sites, bands, caterers, photographers, etc., book their calendars this early, if not earlier. If you have a year between your engagement and your wedding, you will also have enough time to make decisions about many other details without feeling too pressured. Be aware, however, that regardless of how much advanced planning you do, you will be spending a significant amount of time on last-minute details during the months just before your wedding, such as addressing your invitations, going to dress fittings, and determining the seating arrangements for your guests. In every stage of your planning, try to focus on the purpose of your gathering, which is the celebration of your love and marriage. This may sound like an obvious goal, but you can easily lose yourselves in the flurry of all the details. One way to keep your focus is to work on planning your ceremony.

In addition to the normal wedding preparations, you, as an interfaith couple, must ask yourselves questions that same-faith couples do not, such as: What does my faith mean to me? How comfortable or uncomfortable am I with my partner's faith and traditions? If we choose to have children, how will we raise them? How will our parents respond to our marriage and to our religious choices? If we choose one faith for the children, will the partner whose religion was not chosen feel left out? How will we celebrate the holidays in our home?

These are difficult questions to answer because they reach into our hearts in ways that defy logic. I have never met a couple, for example, who lost sleep over their theological differences about the nature of God. But I have met many couples who cannot decide how they will raise the children, not because they are observant Jews and Christians, but because they feel guilty or just uneasy about choosing one faith over the other.

If you are struggling over this question about how you will raise your children, you are not alone. This is usually the most difficult question that interfaith couples must answer. It is especially difficult when both partners are strongly identified with their traditions and faith. If you choose one faith for your children, one of you must accept the fact that your children will not be raised with the traditions and beliefs so familiar and dear to you. How, for example, will you feel if your child has a bat mitzvah, but no first communion? What will happen if you have a Christmas tree in your home? How would you feel about bringing Jesus into your children's lives? How would you feel if you children did not know Jesus in the way you do? Whatever decision you make, it is certain that holidays will not be exactly the same as they were when you were growing up.

Many couples want to postpone the decision of faith for their family until their first child is born. I urge you not to do this. In my experience this decision gets more, not less, difficult over time. The real issue is not the children but your relationship. Ultimately, your children will follow whatever path you choose for them, at least for the first several years of their lives. What is it that is preventing you from coming to terms with this decision now? Are you afraid of your partner's or your family's reactions, or are you simply not sure what you yourself want? It is important to answer these and related questions so that you do not begin your marriage with a major unresolved issue.

If you do choose one faith for your children and that faith is not yours, you will experience a sense of loss, and you may fear, as many do, that this choice will leave you out of a major part of your family's life. While it is true that you will not share in the religious life of your children in the same way as your partner, it is also true that your children will not love you less because of this difference. Show them and teach them about your beliefs and traditions. They will enjoy learning and feel closer to you for sharing this time with them. You will also be teaching your children, through your example, that people of different faiths can live happy, full, and shared family lives.

Of course, raising your children in one faith is not your only option. You may decide to raise them in both traditions or to let them make their own choice as they grow older. While I have my own biases about each option, I know that any one of these choices can lead to a very close and happy family life, if both you and your partner fully support the decision you make.

For more information and help dealing with this and other interfaith family life issues, I recommend that you talk to other interfaith couples and that you read some books on interfaith families. *The Intermarriage Handbook,* by Jim Remsen and Judy Petsonk (New York: Morrow, 1998), has been particularly helpful for some couples I have married and counseled. Many Reform Jewish congregations and organizations also sponsor interfaith programs for couples who want to explore these issues. Check with your local Reform rabbis and Jewish community organizations for information about programs in your area. If you like surfing the Internet, I also recommend that you visit some interfaith Web sites. They will lead you to some additional interfaith resources.

As you read and talk with others, you will discover that your conversations about interfaith issues will not end with your decision about the children or with the end of your wedding. This is not something to be feared, but welcomed as a normal part of your life. You may celebrate holidays one way this year and a different way next year. You will continue to explore and experiment until you find just the right expression for you. Remember that all of life is an ongoing process.

From Your Parents' Perspective

Your wedding day is as emotional for your parents as it is for you, but for obviously different reasons. They will rejoice in your happiness, but they may feel some nostalgia and some sense of loss as they watch you pledge your love to your partner, confirming that you are not a child anymore. They will remember their own wedding day and reflect on their life together, on the good and the bad. They will be anxious about all the details of the wedding; if they are divorced, they may feel anxious about seeing each other. And the list goes on. With so much stress, it is not unusual for tensions to rise and for family members to behave in ways that you have never seen before. Try to keep in mind that this is mostly situational stress and will likely subside immediately following the wedding.

One wedding stress you can alleviate is your parents' anxiety about the ceremony itself. Both families are usually anxious about the ceremony because they do not know what to expect. They wonder: Will the ceremony be balanced, representing both sides equally? Will the unfamiliar elements be explained so we don't feel alienated? Will the rabbi, priest, minister, or officiant say something that will offend us? Will the ceremony honor us and be sensitive to our history, customs, and beliefs? These are normal questions and concerns. You can calm your parents' fears by showing them a draft of your ceremony. They almost always feel relieved when they see the text because now they know there will be no surprises; and in the very rare event that your parents do object strongly to some part of the service, you have time to edit, if you wish.

Understanding the Jewish Response to Jesus

One element that is not usually included in interfaith ceremonies are prayers said in Jesus' name. It is not easy for many Christians to understand why many Jews react so negatively to these prayers. After all, wasn't Jesus Jewish? Do we not all pray to the same God? Of course the answer to both of these questions is yes, but the problem is more complex. It involves issues of history as well as theology.

For Christians, Jesus is the foundation and focus of their faith. He was and is the messiah, God, and their savior. His teachings, as recorded in the New Testament, are the focus of worship, study, and prayer. But for Jews, Jesus was not a messiah or God, but rather a very human prophet; so, for Jews, it is inappropriate, and even sacrilegious, to say prayers in his name.

In addition to the theological differences, a painful history of Jewish-Christian relations influences the Jewish response to Jesus. Over the centuries, hundreds of thousands of Jews have been killed in the name of Jesus Christ. While this is no longer happening, there are still a few churches teaching their children that Jews are responsible for Jesus' death and that Jews will go to hell because they do not accept Jesus as their savior. There are still churches that tell their children that Jews are lesser human beings, and sometimes evil human beings, because of their different faith. These associations of Jesus with persecution make many Jews feel uncomfortable when hearing his name and when seeing a cross.

If you are a Christian, you may be angry or upset after reading this last paragraph. You might be thinking what many devout Christians have said to me: "But I had nothing to do with the atrocities of the past. My family and my church did not teach me to hate or discriminate against the Jewish people. They taught me to love all people: the essence of Jesus' teaching is love and kindness. Why can't you accept me for my beliefs?"

Your Jewish partner can and does accept you for who you are and what you believe, or you would not be getting married. His/her request to exclude Jesus from the service is truly not personal. Many Jews simply cannot separate Jesus' name from the painful images and memories of the past, because Jewish identity, more so than Christian identity, is tied to history and culture as well as theology. To be Jewish means to feel a part of a family whose roots and loyalties date back to biblical times, and this familial, or cultural, connection is often stronger than any connection they feel toward Jewish theology or religious practice. This explains how and why many men and women proudly identify themselves as Jews even when they rarely attend a synagogue.

As Jewish-Christian relations and understanding continue to improve, as they have over the last few decades, the wounds of the past may heal and Jews and Christians alike will be able to respect and honor each other's traditions without experiencing any lingering discomfort. Until then, the unpleasant fact remains that many Jews feel uneasy seeing a cross or hearing Jesus' name, even when these symbols are important to ones they love.

Most interfaith couples resolve this problem by agreeing to say all prayers in God's name, not in Jesus' name, and by agreeing to hold the ceremony in a chapel or sanctuary in which no crosses are visible. This is acceptable to the Catholic Church and to most ministers who officiate at interfaith ceremonies.

Even though this compromise is common practice, it is important for the Jewish partner to understand what a sacrifice this may be for his or her partner.

Focus on the Celebration of Your Love

Remember, your wedding day is a celebration of your love and your commitment. It is a time of sharing and rejoicing with family and friends. In preparation for your special day, I strongly recommend that during the week before the ceremony you spend some time away from all the details and decisions surrounding your wedding. One couple I married took a weekend trip away the weekend before their wedding. Another couple, who planned their wedding at an out-of-state resort, arrived a couple of days before their guests and used this time to relax and enjoy the sights. If taking time away is not an option for you, consider a simple evening out, with the understanding that you will not talk about any wedding details. Even small, simple breaks from wedding planning can help you be more present and more centered for your wedding day and celebration.

Rabbis, Priests, Ministers, and Other Officiants

✿

Most ministers will perform interfaith weddings, but most rabbis will not. It may also be difficult to find a Catholic priest who can participate (see "The Intermarriage Controversy" section in the introduction for more details). So, if you are looking for a rabbi and/or a priest, I suggest that you begin your search as early as possible.

Finding a Rabbi

First ask friends and relatives for names of those who might be willing to conduct your ceremony. Personal referrals are usually the best. If this is not fruitful, contact the Rabbinic Center for Research and Counseling in Westfield, New Jersey, at 908-233-0419. The Center publishes a nation-wide list of rabbis who will officiate. This list is constantly updated, and it includes some information about each rabbi's requirements.

It is important to know that most of these rabbis will participate only if you agree to raise your children Jewishly and only if they are the sole officiant. Some require you to use a set service, while others will work with you to create your own. Only a few rabbis will co-officiate with a priest or minister. Use the list as a guide, but know that this list is not necessarily complete. If the rabbi you call is unavailable, ask her/him for the names of others in your area who might be able to help you.

If you still cannot find a rabbi, you might try calling the nearest Reform Jewish congregation and ask to talk to the rabbi. If he or she does not perform these ceremonies, ask him/her for names of those who might participate. But be prepared for a rejection and a continued search because, as I mentioned earlier, most rabbis will not participate in interfaith weddings. It may take you several weeks to find a rabbi who will work with you.

Finding a Priest

First call your local pastor and ask him for help. As I mentioned earlier, every priest is obligated by Church law to help couples create a healthy marriage. This includes helping interfaith couples with their weddings. In practice, however, it is often hard to find a priest to participate, especially if you are a nonpracticing Catholic. Some priests are so busy that they literally do not have the time to help; others personally oppose intermarriage. But it is important to know that Church law supersedes a priest's personal feelings. If you are having trouble finding a priest, call the office of the bishop of your diocese, which will help you locate a priest who will officiate.

When you meet with the priest who will be participating in your ceremony, he will tell you about any special dispensations and permissions you will need in order for the Church to recognize and bless your marriage. As a Catholic, you will need a special dispensation to marry a non-Catholic, and you will need special permission to hold your wedding outside the church. If you are creating your own ceremony, you may also need a Dispensation from Canonical Form, and the priest himself will need special permission to participate in your ceremony if it is held outside his own parish. Do not worry, however, about obtaining these papers; they are mostly formalities that your priest will handle for you.

There is one misconception about the Catholic Church that is important to dispel. Many interfaith couples believe that they must promise to raise their children as Catholics in order to have their marriage blessed by the Church. This is *not* true. Of course, the Church would prefer that you raise your children as Catholics, just as a rabbi would prefer that you raise your children as Jews. It is true that according to canon law, a priest must inform the Catholic partner that the Church expects him or her to do everything in his or her power to have the children baptized and raised as Catholics; and the Church's expectation must be made clear to the Jewish partner. But as an interfaith couple, you are not required to sign a document promising to raise your children as Catholics, and you cannot be denied permission to have your marriage blessed by the Church if you choose to raise your children as Jews. For a fuller explanation of church policies and expectations, talk to a priest.

Working with a Rabbi and a Priest or Minister

If you want a rabbi and a priest or minister to conduct your ceremony, you need to start your search earlier than most. Only a few clergy will co-officiate, and these few fill their calendars quickly. Calling those you'd like to have officiate at your wedding a year in advance is not too early. When you do find the right people, the rest of your work is easy.

Typically, your rabbi and priest or minister do not need to meet face-to-face. All of their coordination can be done by phone. When you meet individually with them, they will explain their own process and expectations, and they will share their ceremony resources and experiences with you. As you discuss the details of your wedding, I also encourage you to share this book with them. Together, you will decide how you will create your ceremony.

Many couples fear that the rabbi and priest or minister will argue or struggle over various aspects of the wedding, but such conflict is rare. Those who agree to co-officiate usually understand the needs and sensibilities of interfaith couples and audiences. This is especially true for those who have experience performing interfaith ceremonies.

When both a rabbi and a priest or minister lead a service, they usually divide the parts they perform equally between them. The rabbi conducts the particularly Jewish elements, such as the blessing over the wine and the breaking of the glass; the priest or minister leads the specifically Christian elements, such as a New Testament reading and the lighting of a unity candle. Priests/ministers usually preside over the exchange of vows and rabbis typically lead the exchange of rings. This is so because the vows are considered the most important part of many Christian weddings, and the ring exchange is considered the most important part of a Jewish ceremony. The passages that are not specifically Jewish or Christian are divided equally between the two clergy persons.

Other Officiants

Rabbis, priests, and ministers are not the only ones who can legally officiate at weddings. Justices of the peace also have the authority to do so, and
they are often receptive to working with couples on a service that meets
their unique needs. If you are interested in having a justice of the peace
perform your wedding, call the town clerk's office in the town in which
you are getting married and ask them for the names and telephone numbers of justices in their area.

In some states, like Massachusetts, you may also be able to have a
friend or relative officiate at your ceremony and sign your marriage
license. This is possible by obtaining permission for a One-day Solem-
nization. By filling out a form and paying a small fee, any citizen of the
state can be authorized to officiate. To find out whether this option is
available to you in the state in which you are getting married, call any
town clerk's office in that state. They should be able to provide you with
this information.

Clergy Fees

Most rabbis and many ministers will charge you a fee for officiating at
your ceremony. Some priests and ministers prefer to ask you to make a
donation to their church or organization in return for their services. The
amount of these fees and donations varies greatly from city to city and
from one clergy person to the next, ranging from tens of dollars to over a
thousand dollars. There are many reasons for the differences in fees,
including the different financial structures and expectations of each religious community. The factors are too numerous and varied to address
here. As you speak to potential officiants, you will learn what the average
fees are in your area.

Remember, however, when you are considering the fees and donations, that your rabbi, priest, or minister is giving you much more time
than the few minutes he/she officiates. With premarital counseling and
meetings, rehearsals, ceremony preparations, and wedding-day travel
and festivities, rabbis, priests, and ministers spend many hours on each

wedding. Just keep this in mind when you are writing out your check(s) for them.

Justice of the Peace Fees

Justices of the peace usually charge a modest fee that is set by the state. In Massachusetts, for example, the fee for 1998 is less than fifty dollars. Know, however, that these set fees apply to performing the ceremony only. A justice of the peace can charge you more for other services, such as ceremony preparation, rehearsals, and counseling.

Premarital Counseling

Many rabbis, priests, and ministers are now requiring couples to take some form of a premarital preparation or counseling program. The purpose of these programs is not to focus solely on religious issues. They are designed to give couples an opportunity, in a supportive environment, to look at various aspects of their relationship, including their similar and different needs, communication styles, family backgrounds, etc. The idea is to help couples become more aware of the dynamics of their relationship, of their strengths and weaknesses. This type of awareness is key to building a strong, healthy relationship. Love is wonderful, but love is not enough to sustain a happy marriage. How you live with each other day to day, how you communicate and care for one another, will determine the strength and depth of your bond. Good counseling is an investment in your future and insurance for a long, growing, and deepening relationship.

Many couples are afraid to do this work, especially when they have never been in therapy. They are afraid that the counselor will focus only on their struggles and differences and, in so doing, take some of the romance and spontaneity out of their relationship. This is not the goal of premarital counseling. As I practice it and know it, premarital counseling is a short process meant to strengthen the relationship. It is not in-depth therapy. It includes a few time-limited meetings. The purpose is not to focus on the weaknesses of the relationship, but to help couples begin their marriage with some knowledge and skills that will enhance their life together. This does involve talking about you, about your strengths and weaknesses, likes and dislikes, communication styles and family backgrounds, but with the intention of helping you see and understand each other better before you get married. Most couples find these sessions validating and affirming of their love and their commitment. For the minority who do encounter some serious unresolved issues, they, too, benefit by having the opportunity to address them before they get married.

There are many forms and types of premarital counseling. The Catholic Church provides it through its pre-Cana program. Although most of the other churches and synagogues do not offer a similar class, they usually have a referral list of counselors and organizations that provide premarital counseling. With the divorce rate as high as it is today, all religious communities have taken a greater interest in helping couples engage in some premarital guidance. Check with your clergy for names and resources for it. This counseling may be one of the best investments you, as a couple, make in your life together.

Marriage Licenses

In-state Marriage Licenses

To obtain a marriage license, call your town or city hall and ask for the department that handles marriage licenses. This is usually the clerk's office. They will tell you the steps you must take to get one. I will not go into the specifics here because license fees and requirements vary from state to state. In general, however, the fees are usually less than thirty dollars and most states will ask both of you to appear in person to apply for your license. Only a few states, such as Massachusetts, still require blood tests for venereal diseases. Most states will grant you your license on the same day you apply for it, assuming that you have all the necessary information and test results with you.

In most states, you may apply for your license in one city and hold your wedding in another city or town in your state. Just remember that the town that issues your license will be the town that officially records your marriage. If, for example, you get your license from Boston city hall, but your wedding is held in Amherst, Massachusetts, your marriage will be officially recorded in Boston, not Amherst. Do not worry if this sounds a bit confusing. Your town or city official will go over all the details with you.

Out-of-state Licenses

If you are planning an out-of-state wedding, you must obtain your license from the state in which you are getting married. In this case, call the city or town hall nearest your wedding site for all the details.

Out-of-state Clergy

If you are bringing in your rabbi, priest, or minister from another state to conduct your ceremony, check to see if he or she needs a special license in order to officiate. Many states, like Rhode Island and Connecticut, do not require any special papers. New Hampshire, on the other hand, requires out-of-state clergy to obtain a special license from the secretary of state for each wedding he or she performs. Since each state sets its own rules, it is important to find out what these rules are for the state where your wedding will take place.

Who Signs the Marriage License?

Your rabbi, priest, minister, or justice of the peace is the one authorized to sign your marriage license. He or she is also responsible for sending the document back to the town or city from which it was issued. If you are having both a rabbi and a priest or minister officiating, you need to know that you may not be able to have both sign your license. In Massachusetts, for example, only one name is supposed to appear on the document. If these details are important to you and you want a hand in the decision-making process, check with your city or town hall for clarification.

Obtaining Copies of Your Marriage License

Many states do *not* automatically provide you with a copy of your license. They will do so only upon request and for a small fee. This means that your clergy may not have any paper to give you to confirm that your marriage is legal. The only way you will know it is official is if you call your town or city hall and ask them if they have received the license. It is a good idea to request an official copy. You may need it as proof of a change in your name and for other legal matters.

Interfaith Wedding Ceremonies

This chapter is designed to acquaint you with the basic elements and customs of an interfaith wedding ceremony. It includes a description of different types of ceremonies as well as a detailed outline and explanation of one common order of service.

Types of Interfaith Ceremonies

Interfaith ceremonies can vary greatly in style and content. You will draw on your own beliefs and customs when choosing which style is the right one for you. In general, both Christian and Jewish ceremonies have certain elements in common. They each begin with a greeting of the guests and some opening blessing of the couple. This is followed by an exchange of vows, exchange of rings, pronouncement or declaration of the marriage, and a closing reading or benediction. Of course, each tradition treats these elements differently, and each includes its own unique details.

How you blend these different elements and customs will depend on you, on your faith, and on your feelings and ties to your families and your traditions. Some couples decide to include equal elements from both traditions; others choose to use a basic Jewish ceremony or Christian ceremony, with some minor changes. But one element that is not usually included in Jewish-Christian weddings are prayers said in Jesus' name (see "Understanding the Jewish Response to Jesus" in the first chapter).

JEWISH-STYLE AND
JEWISH-CHRISTIAN CEREMONIES

In this book I focus on two types of interfaith ceremonies; one is a Jewish-style ceremony and the other is a Jewish-Christian ceremony.

A Jewish-style ceremony is a service that includes few, if any, Christian customs or passages. All the basic elements of a Jewish ceremony are present, with the exception of those words and passages that imply that both the bride and groom are Jewish. The standard Jewish ring exchange, for example, says: "Be consecrated to me as my wife/husband, according the laws of Moses and Israel." This exchange is known as the *Haray Aht*. In my opinion, it would be inappropriate for an interfaith couple to say these words because the wedding is not being performed according to the laws of Moses and Israel as they are understood by the majority of Jews. This type of service is popular with couples when the non-Jewish partner has no strong affiliation or identity with any church. See Part II, "Sample Ceremonies," for examples. When the Jewish partner has a weak connection to his or her heritage, the ceremony may be predominately Catholic or Protestant, with few Jewish components. If you are interested in one of these ceremonies, ask your priest or minister for examples and guidance.

Jewish-Christian ceremonies include elements from both traditions. These services can vary greatly, but most include the following:

From the Jewish side . . .
Some Hebrew blessings, along with the English translation or interpretation; the blessing over the wine; a special set of seven wedding blessings, recited in Hebrew and English; the breaking of the glass; and the use of a *huppah* (wedding canopy). An interfaith *ketubah*, or wedding covenant, is also signed before the ceremony. (See "The Interfaith Ketubah" in this chapter for more details.)

From the Christian side . . .
Two biblical readings, one from the Hebrew Scriptures, known as the Torah to Jews, and one from the New Testament. The most widely used New Testament passage is from the first letter of Paul to the Corinthians, chapter 13, which speaks about the nature of love. The service also

includes the lighting of a unity candle, which symbolizes the lives of two individuals uniting in marriage; the declaration of consent, which asks the couple if they are coming to the marriage of their own free will and if they promise to love and honor one another; and one or more prayers from the standard liturgy that are adapted for the occasion.

The Length of the Ceremony

The average length of a Jewish ceremony is twenty minutes. A Catholic ceremony, when it is part of mass, runs about an hour. Most interfaith ceremonies run between twenty and forty minutes. (See the ceremonies in Part II for examples.)

The Interfaith Ketubah

Fifteen to thirty minutes before the ceremony begins, couples often sign an interfaith ketubah.

A traditional ketubah is a Jewish religious document that is signed by the bride, groom, and at least two witnesses immediately before the wedding ceremony. Originally, it was a legal document that detailed some of the rights and obligations of the bride and groom. Like many prenuptial agreements, it talked much about property rights but never mentioned a word about a couple's love and commitment. We do not know exactly when this custom began, but it is at least as old as the first century of the common era. Its original purpose, like a prenuptial agreement, was to offer some protection, in this case for the bride, in the event of divorce. Given the era in which it was written, it was quite an extraordinary document because it gave some legal rights to women in an age when women had few rights.

Today, *ketubot* (the plural form of ketubah) have taken on new forms and meanings. Most are now spiritual covenants, not legal documents, that the bride and the groom make with each other, although some couples still choose to sign the ancient traditional text. The new ketubot include the English and Hebrew date and place of the wedding, as well as some expression of the couple's spiritual and emotional commitment to each other. The ketubah may end with a blessing, followed by places for the signatures of the couple and at least two witnesses. Traditionally witnesses could not be relatives of the bride and groom, nor could they be women, but today, most Reform and many Conservative rabbis will allow anyone the couple chooses to serve as a witness.

An interfaith ketubah contains the same elements as listed above, but the text either acknowledges the different traditions of the couple or is so general that it could be used for a Jewish or interfaith couple. (See Appendix II for examples.)

Ketubot vary greatly in style, content, and price; and you can find them displayed at most Jewish bookstores and gift shops. If you only see standard Jewish texts, do not be discouraged; many shops do not display interfaith documents. Ask the clerks if they have interfaith texts; and if they say they do not, take down the name and number of the artists who have created the traditional ketubot. Many of them have interfaith ketubot for sale. If they do not, they will most likely know other artists who do.

Before you decide to buy a ketubah, however, talk to your rabbi. He or she may have certain requirements for the text.

The Huppah, or Wedding Canopy

Many interfaith couples choose to exchange their vows under a huppah. A huppah is a Jewish wedding canopy that usually consists of four poles or posts with a tallis (Jewish prayer shawl), a decorative cloth, or greenery suspended between them. The canopy must be large enough to suggest a home or shelter. This means that a floral arch or trellis does not qualify as a huppah. There are no rules about the exact size of the canopy, but it should be large enough for the bride and groom, the rabbi, and the priest or minister, to stand beneath it. The rest of the wedding party stands to either side.

At one time, the huppah was the marriage tent or room in which the bride and groom consummated their marriage. Today the huppah has many meanings. It primarily symbolizes God's presence and the new home the couple will create together. The sides of the canopy remain open, reminiscent of Abraham's hospitality, a symbol of the importance of the couple's involvement with their general community and with their family and friends. Modern writer and poet Debra Cash wrote a lovely poem called "The Succah and the Huppah" that captures the multi-faceted beauty of the huppah today. Her poem is included in Part III, "Menu of Passages," under "Explanation of the Huppah."

The huppah may be freestanding or handheld. The handheld huppah is made of four six- to seven-foot-long poles with a tallis or decorative cloth suspended between them. Holding one of the poles is considered an honor and, although traditional Jews restrict who is permitted to be a huppah holder, most rabbis who perform interfaith weddings welcome anyone a couple chooses for this honor.

You can easily make your own huppah by suspending any cloth between four poles. One couple I married asked friends to make something they could attach or sew onto the cloth and then covered their huppah with these personalized mementos. Another couple used a plain linen cloth that was a family heirloom. You may want to consider a special huppah for your wedding. They can make wonderful keepsakes that can be handed down from generation to generation.

If you do not have the time or inclination to make your own huppah, you may be able to borrow one from a synagogue, or you can often rent one from a Jewish bookstore or gift shop. Florists can also make a huppah for you.

The Order and Content of the Ceremony

The order of an interfaith service can vary, but most follow this general outline:

1. Opening Remarks
2. Explanation of the Huppah
3. Acknowledging Loved Ones Who Have Died
4. Acknowledging Your Two Traditions
5. General Marriage Blessings and Prayers
6. Remarks by the Officiant
7. Readings (biblical and/or secular)
8. The Blessing over the Wine
9. Affirmation of the Families and of the Guests

10. Exchange of Vows (including Declaration of Intent and Consent, when applicable)
11. Exchange of Rings
12. Lighting the Unity Candle
13. The Seven Wedding Blessings
14. The Pronouncement
15. Kiss
16. Closing Reading(s) and/or Benediction
17. Explanation of the *Yichud*
18. Breaking of the Glass
19. Kiss

Of course, you may not wish to include all of these elements—you may choose to add something that is not listed here—but this is one very common order of service. To see how this order and these elements differ from traditional services, turn to Appendix I, "Traditional Wedding Ceremonies." That section includes the entire texts of typical Reform Jewish, Roman Catholic, Episcopal, and Presbyterian services.

Now let's take a more detailed look at each of the elements of an interfaith ceremony.

OPENING REMARKS

The opening words of your ceremony set the tone of your service. They usually include a greeting of the guests and a statement about the purpose of your gathering. Many couples like to begin informally, such as:

> Welcome family and friends. We are gathered together to celebrate (bride) and (groom)'s love for each other and their decision to make a lifelong commitment of marriage to one another . . .

Others like to start with words from their traditional liturgies. The following is an example from the Episcopal *Book of Common Prayer*:

> Dearly Beloved: we have come together in the presence of God to witness and bless the joining of this man and this

woman in Holy Matrimony. The bond and covenant of marriage was established by God and humankind . . .

There are yet other couples who like to open their ceremony with a mix of traditional and contemporary passages. You will find more examples of each style in the "Menu of Passages" in Part III.

EXPLANATION OF THE HUPPAH

If you are using a huppah, it is a good idea to explain its meaning at the beginning of your service. Some couples like simple explanations; others like more historical and detailed versions. You will find examples of both in "Explanation of the Huppah," in Part III.

ACKNOWLEDGING LOVED ONES WHO HAVE DIED

Your wedding day will stir up many emotions, which may include some grief about loved ones who have died and some sadness that they cannot be with you on your special day. Instead of pushing their memories aside, you can acknowledge them during your ceremony. This is one way to include them, simply and briefly in spirit:

There are those close to (bride/partner) and (groom/partner) who are not here today, but who would rejoice with them if they were. (They especially remember . . .) Let us think of them now in a moment of silence.

You may wish to mention your loved ones by name, but think carefully about this. Saying their names may bring up too much grief. Let your heart and intuition be your guide. (See "Remembering Loved Ones Who Have Died" in Part III for more examples.)

ACKNOWLEDGING YOUR TWO TRADITIONS

If you are not using a Jewish-style ceremony, you may wish to say something about the weaving of your Jewish and Christian traditions into the ceremony. Naming the obvious affirms your different faiths and sends a message to everyone that you are proud of your backgrounds and that you embrace both heritages as part of your love and relationship.

One way to address this is as follows:

Out of two different and distinct traditions they have come together to learn the best of what each has to offer, appreciating their differences and confirming that being together is far better than being apart from each other. As we bless this marriage under the huppah, the Jewish symbol of the new home being consummated here, we will later light the unity candle, the Christian symbol of two people becoming one in marriage.

See "Acknowledging Different Traditions" in Part III for more examples.

GENERAL MARRIAGE BLESSINGS AND PRAYERS

What would a wedding ceremony be without one or more blessings and prayers for you and your marriage? The "Menu of Passages" contains many selections from Jewish, Christian, and secular sources. Choose those you like, and use the sample ceremonies as your guides for placement.

REMARKS BY THE OFFICIANT

Remarks refer to the officiant's individualized talk to you. Most clergy speak about the nature of marriage, love, and commitment. The more the people conducting your wedding know you, the more personalized their comments can be. The length of their remarks here will vary depending on the speaker, but most clergy limit their remarks to about five minutes.

READINGS

Readings refer to both biblical and secular passages. You are free to choose as many readings as you like, but I do not recommend more than a few. The readings should add emphasis; they should punctuate, not overshadow the rest of the service. You may insert the readings anywhere you like, but try to fit them into the context of the words or elements that surround them. If, for example, a priest or minister is participating in your ceremony, place his or her remarks immediately following a biblical reading. Christian clergy usually use the scripture readings as a springboard for their homilies.

Christian weddings typically include two biblical readings, one from the Hebrew Bible, or Torah, and one from the New Testament. For weddings the readings focus on love and relationship, but there are surprisingly few of these passages to choose from. Let's take a look at those you may find appropriate.

Biblical Readings

The story about Eve's creation from Adam's rib is one of the most frequently used Hebrew scripture readings, but I personally try to avoid this passage because it implies that Eve was made to serve Adam. I prefer what is known as the first creation story, which is found in the first book of Genesis. In this story, Adam and Eve are created equally and at the same time, as you can see:

> And God created man and woman in His/Her image, male and female God created them. God blessed them both and said to them: "Be fruitful and increase, fill the earth and master it; and rule the fish of the sea, the birds of the sky, and all the living things that creep on earth."
>
> (Genesis 1:27–28)

Two other popular Hebrew scripture, or Torah, readings are from Hosea and Ruth.

> And I shall betroth you unto me forever,
> I will betroth you unto me in righteousness,
> And in loving kindness and in compassion;
> And I shall betroth you unto me in faithfulness.
>
> (Hosea 2:19)

> Wherever you go, I will go; wherever you lodge, I will lodge; your people will be my people, and your God my God.
>
> (Ruth 1:16)

The New Testament passage quoted most frequently is from the first letter of Paul to the Corinthians, chapter 12:31–13:8a:

If I have all the eloquence of men (and women) or of angels, but speak without love, I am simply a gong booming or a cymbal clashing.

If I have the gift of prophecy, understanding all mysteries and knowing everything, and if I have all faith so as to move mountains, but am without love, I gain nothing.

If I give away all I possess, and if I deliver my body to be burned, but am without love, I gain nothing. [Because of its graphic content, this verse is often excluded for wedding ceremonies.]

Love is always patient and kind; it is never jealous nor selfish, it does not take offense and is not resentful.

Love takes not pleasure in other people's sins, but delights in the truth. It is always ready to excuse, to trust, and to endure whatever comes. Love does not end.

There are in the end three things that last: Faith, Hope and Love, and the greatest of these is Love.

The Lord's Prayer is sometimes included in interfaith weddings; but since it is considered to be the most basic Christian prayer, many Jews feel uncomfortable reciting it. You and your partner should talk to each other to determine whether reading this prayer would feel appropriate for your ceremony.

Our Father in heaven, hallowed be Your Name,
Your kingdom come, Your will be done, on earth as in heaven.

Give us today our daily bread.
Forgive us our sins, as we forgive those who sin against us.

Save us from the time of trial, and deliver us from evil.
For the kingdom, the power, and the glory are Yours, now
and forever. Amen.

These are some basic readings. See Part IV, "Wedding Readings," for a wider selection.

Secular Readings

You may wish to include one or more love poems or readings in your ceremony. There are countless possibilities, everything from Shakespeare to Rainer Maria Rilke. Which you choose will depend on your personal tastes. See Part IV, "Wedding Readings," for a sampling of some popular passages that have been used in wedding ceremonies I have performed.

THE BLESSING OVER THE WINE

The blessing over the wine, known as the kiddush, is a part of most Jewish celebrations and holidays. The word *kiddush* means sanctification; so, in a sense, the wedding is sanctified with this blessing.

The blessing over the wine is usually recited twice during a Jewish ceremony, once as part of the seven traditional wedding blessings and again, separately, during another section of the service. Historically, these two cups of wine represent two different aspects of a Jewish wedding, the betrothal and the marriage itself. For interfaith ceremonies, you can choose to recite the blessing once or twice. If you include two blessings, the first is usually recited before your exchange of vows and rings and the second is read after your exchanges as part of the seven wedding blessings. See the sample ceremonies in Part II for examples of the use of one and two cups of wine and their placement in the ceremony.

An explanation of the symbolism of the wine often precedes the blessing. The following is an example taken from Reform liturgy:

> This cup of wine is symbolic of the cup of life. As you share the one cup of wine, you undertake to share all that the future may bring. All the sweetness life's cup may hold for you should be sweeter because you drink it together; whatever drops of bitterness it may contain should be less bitter because you share them.
>
> As I recite the blessing over the wine, we pray that God will bestow fullness of joy upon you.

בָּרוּךְ אַתָּה יְיָ אֱלֹהֵינוּ מֶלֶךְ הָעוֹלָם בּוֹרֵא פְּרִי הַגָּפֶן.

Blessed are You, O Lord our God, Creator of the fruit of the vine.

See "Blessing over the Wine" in Part III for more selections of introductions and explanations of the blessing over the wine.

The wine cup(s) itself, known as the kiddush cup, may be made of any material. Traditionally, it is a silver goblet that can be engraved with your names and the date of your wedding, or with an expression of love, such as this popular passage from the Song of Songs: "I am my beloved's and my beloved is mine" (in Hebrew and/or English).

What type of wine do you drink? Traditionally the wine is a sweet kosher red wine, but most rabbis will allow you to use any wine you wish. Most people associate kosher wine with Manischewitz's sweet concord grape variety, but kosher wine now comes in many varieties, including some nice white chardonnays. I mention this because many brides feel safer using white rather than red wine, just in case they spill some on their dress! Regardless of the vintage, I recommend that you choose a wine that has at least a touch of sweetness in it, since the wine not only sanctifies your day, but it also implies a prayer for the sweetness everyone wishes for you in your married life.

AFFIRMATION OF THE FAMILIES AND OF THE GUESTS

Family vows stem from a Protestant tradition known as the affirmation of the family and the congregation. During this portion of the ceremony, the minister asks the family and the guests if they are willing to support the couple in their marriage. One version of the affirmation is as follows:

Priest:
Do you, the family and friends of (bride) and (groom), give your blessing to them and promise to do everything in your power to uphold them in their marriage?

Guests:
We give our blessing and promise our loving support.

While a Protestant tradition, this is a nice way for those of many faiths to acknowledge and include everyone present in the wedding ceremony.

EXCHANGE OF VOWS

The exchange of vows is the most important part of the ceremony in the eyes of many Christian leaders. Consequently, participating priests and ministers often request, or insist on, leading this part of this service. The exact form of the vows, however, can vary. As an interfaith couple, you are not required to say any particular combination of words. Most rabbis, priests, and ministers will permit you to use any vows you wish, including those you write on your own. If you are Catholic, however, you may need to get a special Dispensation from Canonical Form in order to use the vows you write.

The following exchange, called the Declaration of Consent or Intent, is familiar to most Catholics and Protestants:

Priest:
(Bride) and (groom), have you come here freely and without reservations to give yourselves to each other in marriage?

Bride and groom:
We have.

Priest:
(Bride) and (groom), since it is your intention to enter into marriage, join your right hands and repeat after me.

Bride and groom:
In the name of God, I, (bride/groom), take you, (groom/bride), to be my husband/wife, to have and to hold from this day forward, for better for worse, for richer for poorer, in sickness and in health, to love and to cherish, until we are parted by death. This is my solemn vow.

For a sampling of a wide variety of vows, turn to "Vows" in Part III.

EXCHANGE OF RINGS

While the exchange of vows is considered one of the most important elements in Catholic and Protestant ceremonies, the ring exchange is viewed as one of the most important parts of a Jewish ceremony. The traditional Jewish exchange, known as the Haray Aht, is considered by many Jews to be the distinguishing feature of a Jewish ceremony. The following is the traditional Hebrew Haray Aht along with the English translation.

הֲרֵי אַתְּ מְקוּדֶשֶׁת (אַתָּה מְקֻדָּשׁ) לִי בְּטַבַּעַת זוּ כְּדַת מֹשֶׁה
וְיִשְׂרָאֵל.

With this ring be consecrated to me as my wife/husband, according to the heritage of Moses and Israel.

While this traditional formula of the Haray Aht is well known, many Jewish couples today are choosing their own, more personal words for their ring exchange. Most interfaith couples do not use the Haray Aht because the phrase "according to the heritage of Moses and Israel" implies that both partners are Jewish. However, be aware that some rabbis will refuse to officiate unless you agree to recite this traditional ring exchange as is. If you want a Jewish-style ceremony and like the basic feel of this traditional exchange, you can change the last words to reflect your own beliefs:

With this ring be consecrated to me as my wife/husband, in the spirit of our tradition(s) and in the eyes of God.

See "Ring Exchanges" in Part III for more examples of words you might say as you exchange your rings.

It is also an old Jewish custom for the bride and groom to first place the wedding ring each other's index finger. According to one ancient belief, the index finger is connected to a special artery that leads directly to the heart. By placing the ring here, the couple symbolically join their hearts to each other. After the ring exchange, both the bride and groom switch the ring to their ring finger. Many couples today like the rich symbolism of this custom and choose to include it in their ceremony.

LIGHTING THE UNITY CANDLE

The lighting of a unity candle is a common feature in many Christian ceremonies. There are actually three candles used in this ritual, two small candles and one large candle. The two smaller candles symbolize the individual lives of the bride and groom. Until their wedding day, each has let their light shine independently within their communities. Now, as part of their wedding ceremony, they light the larger candle with the two smaller candles to symbolize their new union of marriage. This does not mean that they lose their individuality, but that, in marriage, they form a new, unique, and powerful single bond.

The couple's mothers often light the two small candles at the beginning of the ceremony, after they process down the aisle. This is lovely symbolism—the parents light a candle to represent their child, the life they brought into this world. Then the bride and groom each take the light given to them by their parents to light a new flame of their own.

Although lighting candles is not traditionally a part of a Jewish wedding, there is some precedent for such a practice. According to one Jewish teaching, light represents joy, so if you increase the amount of light at your ceremony by lighting candles, you symbolically add to the joy of your wedding. There is a quote from a famous mystical rabbi who lived centuries ago that fits very nicely into a candle-lighting ceremony. The rabbi's name was the Baal Shem Tov. He once said:

> From every human being there rises a light that reaches straight to heaven. And when two souls are destined to find one another, their two streams of light flow together and a single brighter light goes forth from their united being.

See "The Unity Candle" in Part III for different ways to introduce and explain the candle lighting.

THE SEVEN WEDDING BLESSINGS

A special set of seven wedding blessings, known as the *Sheva Berachot* in Hebrew, has been a part of Jewish weddings for centuries. Six of the seven are prescribed in the Talmud, or Jewish codes, which were written around 500 C.E. A seventh blessing, the blessing over the wine, was added later in the sixth century.

The number seven is significant because it represents the seven days of creation, or the six days God created the world and the seventh day on which God rested. Symbolically, seven is a number of completion, of perfection. According to Jewish lore, when two people fall in love, they help each other feel more complete and more whole than they ever felt alone.

The seven blessings praise God for:

1. Creating the fruit of the vine: the blessing over the wine, or kiddush
2. Creating the earth and all that is in it
3. Creating humanity
4. Creating man and woman in God's image
5. The miracle of birth
6. Bringing the bride and groom together to rejoice and live in harmony as did the first couple, Adam and Eve
7. The joy of the bride and groom and the hope for a world that will one day be filled with the joy of lovers and the laughter of children.

Notice that only the last two of the seven blessings refer specifically to the bride and groom. The blessings build from the general to the specific, from God's creation of the world, to the creation of humanity, to the creation of man and woman, to the bearing of children and perpetuation of life, to the rejoicing of this one couple, and finally to the hopes and joys of the couple and their guests for a peaceful world.

Traditionally, these blessings are chanted or sung in Hebrew and then read in English.

בָּרוּךְ אַתָּה יְיָ אֱלֹהֵינוּ מֶלֶךְ הָעוֹלָם בּוֹרֵא פְּרִי הַגָּפֶן.

We praise you, O Lord our God, Ruler of the universe, Creator of the fruit of the vine.

בָּרוּךְ אַתָּה יְיָ אֱלֹהֵינוּ מֶלֶךְ הָעוֹלָם שֶׁהַכֹּל בָּרָא לִכְבוֹדוֹ.

We praise you, O Lord our God, Ruler of the universe, Creator of all things for your glory.

בָּרוּךְ אַתָּה יְיָ אֱלֹהֵינוּ מֶלֶךְ הָעוֹלָם יוֹצֵר הָאָדָם.

We praise you, O Lord our God, Ruler of the universe, Creator of man and woman.

בָּרוּךְ אַתָּה יְיָ אֱלֹהֵינוּ מֶלֶךְ הָעוֹלָם, אֲשֶׁר יָצַר אֶת־הָאָדָם בְּצַלְמוֹ, בְּצֶלֶם דְּמוּת תַּבְנִיתוֹ, וְהִתְקִין לוֹ מִמֶּנּוּ בִּנְיַן עֲדֵי עַד בָּרוּךְ אַתָּה יְיָ יוֹצֵר הָאָדָם.

We praise you, O Lord our God, Ruler of the universe, who created man and woman in your image that together they might perpetuate life. We praise you, O God, Creator of man and woman.

שׂוֹשׂ תָּשִׂישׂ וְתָגֵל צִיּוֹן בְּקִבּוּץ בָּנֶיהָ לְתוֹכָהּ בְּשִׂמְחָה. בָּרוּךְ אַתָּה יְיָ מְשַׂמֵּחַ צִיּוֹן בְּבָנֶיהָ.

May Zion rejoice as her children are restored to her in joy. Praised are you, O God, who causes Zion to rejoice at her children's return.

שַׂמֵּחַ תְּשַׂמַּח רֵעִים הָאֲהוּבִים כְּשַׂמֵּחֲךָ יְצִירְךָ בְּגַן עֵדֶן מִקֶּדֶם. בָּרוּךְ אַתָּה יְיָ מְשַׂמֵּחַ חָתָן וְכַלָּה.

We praise you, O Lord, our God, Ruler of the universe, who causes bride and groom to rejoice. May these loving companions rejoice as have your creatures since the days of creation.

בָּרוּךְ אַתָּה יְיָ אֱלוֹהֵינוּ מֶלֶךְ הָעוֹלָם, אֲשֶׁר בָּרָא שָׂשׂוֹן וְשִׂמְחָה, חָתָן וְכַלָּה, גִּילָה רִנָּה דִּיצָה וְחֶדְוָה, אַהֲבָה וְאַחֲוָה, שָׁלוֹם וְרֵעוּת. מְהֵרָה יְיָ אֱלֹהֵינוּ יִשָּׁמַע בְּעָרֵי יְהוּדָה וּבְחוּצוֹת יְרוּשָׁלַיִם, קוֹל שָׂשׂוֹן וְקוֹל שִׂמְחָה, קוֹל חָתָן וְקוֹל כַּלָּה, קוֹל מִצְהֲלוֹת חֲתָנִים מֵחֻפָּתָם וּנְעָרִים מִמִּשְׁתֵּה נְגִינָתָם. בָּרוּךְ אַתָּה יְיָ מְשַׂמֵּחַ חָתָן עִם־הַכַּלָּה.

We praise you, O Lord our God, Ruler of the universe, Creator of joy and gladness, bride and groom, love and kinship, peace and friendship. O God, may there always be heard in the cities of Israel and in the streets of Jerusalem the sounds of joy and of happiness, the voice of the groom and the voice of the bride, the shouts of young people celebrating, and the songs of children at play. We praise you, our God, who causes bride and groom to rejoice together.

These seven wedding blessings have been translated and interpreted in many ways. See "The Seven Jewish Wedding Blessings" in Part III for over a dozen different renditions.

THE PRONOUNCEMENT

During the pronouncement, you are declared husband and wife. Most people believe that the officiant must say "Now, by the power vested in me . . ." in order for their marriage to be legal and binding, but this is not true. You may use any words you like. It is not the words, but the officiant's signature on the license that makes the marriage official. Some couples prefer to be married with these words:

By the power of your love and by the commitment you have made, you are now husband and wife.

See "Pronouncement" in Part III for more examples.

CLOSING READING(S) AND/OR BENEDICTION

The benediction, or final blessing, can take many forms, but for interfaith ceremonies the most common concluding blessing is the priestly benediction. It is taken from the Torah, or Hebrew Scripture, and is a standard part of both Christian and Jewish liturgies.

יְבָרֶכְךָ יְיָ וְיִשְׁמְרֶךָ.

May God bless you and keep you.

יָאֵר יְיָ פָּנָיו אֵלֶיךָ וִיחֻנֶּךָּ.

May God's presence shine upon you and be gracious to you.

יִשָּׂא יְיָ פָּנָיו אֵלֶיךָ וְיָשֵׂם לְךָ שָׁלוֹם.

May God's presence be with you and give you peace.
(Numbers 6:24–27)

This is a nice way to end the ceremony, on a note of common prayer and practice. When the service is co-officiated, the rabbi often recites the Hebrew and the priest or minister responds with the English. See "Closing Prayers (Benedictions) and Readings" in Part III for more selections of benedictions and closing readings.

EXPLANATION OF THE YICHUD

Yichud is a Hebrew word that literally means union. In a wedding ceremony it refers to a ritual that occurs immediately following the ceremony, when the newlyweds go to a private room to spend a few minutes alone together before they return to greet their guests. Originally, this was the time when the couple was required to consummate their marriage. Today, however, the yichud simply gives the couple an opportunity to acknowledge, privately, the power and significance of the commitment they have just made. It is also here where they share their first food and drink as a married couple.

If you choose to have a yichud, you may wish to ask your rabbi or officiant to explain the custom as part of the ceremony. By doing this, your guests will not be left wondering where you are, and you will help everyone understand and appreciate another aspect of your wedding rituals. The officiant usually explains the custom immediately before the breaking of the glass. After the glass shatters, the ceremony ends and the celebration begins.

BREAKING OF THE GLASS

The breaking of the glass is the most well-known aspect of a Jewish wedding ceremony, and it is usually included in interfaith ceremonies. The custom has many interpretations and explanations.

In the Orthodox tradition, the breaking of the glass symbolizes the destruction of the Temple in 70 C.E. and all the subsequent sufferings of the Jewish people. Even in a moment of such great joy, we are asked to remember that there is still pain and suffering in the world and that we have a responsibility to help relieve some of that pain and suffering.

Although this is the Orthodox Jewish explanation, the breaking of the glass may have originated at a time when people broke glasses to scare away evil spirits from such lucky people as brides and grooms.

Other explanations include: (1) The glass is broken as a symbol of the irrevocable change in the lives of the couple. Marriage is a transforming experience, one that leaves the couple forever changed. (2) The fragility of the glass suggests the frailty of human relationships. The glass is broken to protect the marriage with the implied prayer, "As this glass shatters, so may your marriage never break." (3) The glass is broken as a symbol of the breaking of the hymen. Centuries ago, the groom was required to show a bloody sheet after the first sexual union, a sign that the couple had united and a sign that the bride was a virgin. Needless to say, this explanation rarely appears in modern wedding ceremonies. (4) A new interpretation for interfaith ceremonies is that the glass is broken to symbolize the breaking down of barriers of prejudice and ignorance between people of different cultures and faiths.

You may include one or more of these interpretations in your ceremony. See "Breaking of the Glass" in Part III for several options.

Which Glass Do You Break?

You can break either the wine cup (kiddush cup) you used during your ceremony or a separate glass that you buy for the sole purpose of breaking. One tradition says you should break the kiddush cup as a symbol of the irrevocable change marriage makes in your lives. For many couples, however, breaking the kiddush cup that they used to bless their marriage is just too unsettling.

By far the prevailing custom is to break a separate glass. I recommend using an inexpensive, stemmed wine glass because it is large and easy to break. Some couples like to break a lightbulb because it makes a loud pop when smashed. Personally, I think something is lost in the meaning of the custom when a lightbulb is used.

Who Breaks the Glass?

Traditionally, the man breaks the glass, but today both the bride and groom are given the opportunity to do so. If both of you want to break a glass, I urge you to use two separate glasses. It is too dangerous for two stomping feet to break one glass!

WHEN DO YOU KISS?

This may sound like a silly question, but few written ceremonies indicate when the bride and groom should kiss. I recommend two kisses in the ceremony, once after the pronouncement and again after the breaking of the glass. It is natural to kiss at the moment you are declared husband and wife, and it is natural to kiss again at the very end of the ceremony, when the celebration begins.

More Customs to Consider

The previous section detailed only one of many possible outlines of a ceremony. It does not list all of the customs and rituals that you could include in your wedding-day preparations and ceremony. This section describes a few more Jewish and Christian customs for you to consider.

FROM JEWISH TRADITIONS . . .

The Mikveh

Traditionally, Jewish brides and grooms immersed themselves in a ritual bath, or mikveh, as part of their preparations for marriage. Although few couples practice this custom today, there are an increasing number who are interested in doing some type of ritual immersion that symbolizes their passage from their single life to their married lives together.

Technically, a mikveh can be any natural body of water, such as a lake, river, or ocean. The only stipulation is that the water must not be stagnant. Mikvehs can also be indoor pools that are specially built according to Jewish laws. These facilities are not usually available, however, to interfaith couples.

If you want to include some form of ritual immersion as part of your preparation for marriage, you can use a natural body of water as your mikveh. If this is not possible because of the weather or your location, you can improvise by using an indoor swimming pool. I do not, however, recommend that you use a bathtub or a hot tub because these pools are not large enough to allow you to immerse yourself totally under water without your arms or legs touching the bottom or the sides. The goal of an immersion is to feel yourself totally surrounded by the water, as if you were in the womb.

What do you do at the mikveh or pool? If you would like to follow the traditional Jewish practice, you would each go to your mikveh separately. There you would immerse yourself totally under water two or three times. As you emerge the final time, you would say one or both of these prayers:

בָּרוּךְ אַתָּה יְיָ אֱלֹהֵינוּ מֶלֶךְ הָעוֹלָם אֲשֶׁר קִדְּשָׁנוּ בְּמִצְוֹתָיו וְצִוָּנוּ עַל הַטְּבִילָה.

Praised are you, God of all creation, who sanctifies us with your commandments and commanded us concerning immersion.

בָּרוּךְ אַתָּה יְיָ אֱלֹהֵינוּ מֶלֶךְ הָעוֹלָם שֶׁהֶחֱיָנוּ וְקִיְּמָנוּ וְהִגִּיעָנוּ לַזְּמַן הַזֶּה.

Blessed are you, our God, Ruler of the Universe, who has kept us alive and preserved us and enabled us to reach this joyous time.

While some couples like to follow this traditional procedure, others like to create their own rituals of immersion. One interfaith couple I married, for example, used a nearby lake for their mikveh. While the mikveh itself was kosher (traditional), the ritual they used at the mikveh was unique. The bride asked a few close friends to accompany her to the lake, provide her with some emotional support, and serve as witnesses. There, she immersed herself in the water. As she emerged, her friends gathered around her and gave her their personal blessings. The groom also asked a few of his close friends to serve as witnesses. As he emerged, they gathered around him and told stories about him and about the times they had shared. Both the bride and groom felt this was a very intimate, positive, and powerful spiritual experience, one that helped them mark this important passage in their lives.

If you are interested in a ritual immersion as part of your wedding preparations, talk to your rabbi. He/she will guide you and give you more information about traditional practices and about possible alternatives.

The Bedeken
Bedeken is a Yiddish word meaning covering, and it refers to the custom of veiling the bride. According to the Bible, Jacob was deceived into marrying the wrong woman (Leah) because he did not see his bride's face before the ceremony. The groom veils his bride to symbolically ensure that such a deception does not occur again. As he lowers the veil, this traditional prayer is recited:

אֲחֹתֵנוּ אַתְּ הֲיִי לְאַלְפֵי רְבָבָה. יְשִׂימֵךְ אֱלֹהִים כְּשָׂרָה רִבְקָה רָחֵל וְלֵאָה.

May you be fruitful and prosper. May God make you as Sarah, Rebecca, Rachel, and Leah.

יְבָרֶכְךָ יְיָ וְיִשְׁמְרֶךָ. יָאֵר יְיָ פָּנָיו אֵלֶיךָ וִיחֻנֶּךָּ. יִשָּׂא יְיָ פָּנָיו אֵלֶיךָ וְיָשֵׂם לְךָ שָׁלוֹם.

May God bless you and keep you. May God's presence shine upon and be gracious to you. May God's presence be with you and give you peace.

The bride and groom sign their ketubah immediately before or after the veiling.

Circling
It is a very old Jewish folk custom for the bride to circle the groom during the wedding ceremony. Centuries ago this circle was believed to create an invisible wall of protection for the couple against evil spirits. In more recent times, the circle became symbolic of the couple's new relationship, each now becoming the center of the other's attention.

Traditionally, the bride walks around the groom seven times. Today, many couples choose to walk around each other one to three times as a sign of respect for each other's individuality, as a symbol of their appreciation of their differences, and as a sign of love. The Cabalists, or Jewish mystics, claim that this circling helps the lovers enter the seven spheres of each other's souls.

The circling can occur at any point in the service, but it usually takes place before the actual ceremony begins, or around the exchange of vows. Some couples ask their officiant or friend to read a poem as they are walking.

One couple asked me to read this passage from Hosea as they circled each other:

> I shall betroth you unto me forever,
> I shall betroth you unto me in righteousness,
> And in loving kindness and in compassion;
> And I shall betroth you unto me in faithfulness.

FROM CHRISTIAN TRADITIONS . . .

The Sign of Peace

During many Christian worship services, the priest or minister will ask the members of his/her congregation to turn to those seated near them and give them a sign of peace, such as a handshake or other greeting. Catholic priests traditionally introduce this part of the service by saying:

> Let us offer each other the sign of peace.

As parishoners extend their greetings, they add:

> The peace of Christ be with you.

In interfaith weddings, the priest or minister does not ask the guests to respond in Christ's name, but asks them simply to extend their greetings and well wishes to those seated next to them.

The Priest Blesses the Rings with Holy Water

Many Catholic priests sprinkle the rings with holy water before the bride and groom place the rings on each other's fingers.

The Priest/Minister Wraps the Couple's Hands with His/Her Vestment

As part of the exchange of vows and the pronouncement, some Episcopal priests and Protestant ministers will wrap their vestment around the couple's clasped hands as they offer a blessing.

The Crowning of the Bride and Groom

It is a Greek Orthodox custom to crown both the bride and the groom with a green wreath during the wedding ceremony. The crowns are joined by a ribbon to symbolize that the two are now one. As the priest places the crowns on their heads, he says:

Oh Lord our God, with glory and honor crown them.

A reader then recites the following:

You have set upon their heads crowns of precious stones; they asked life of you, and you gave it to them. For you will give them your blessing forever and ever: you will make them rejoice with gladness through your presence.

As part of this ritual, the best man switches the crowns between the bride and groom to acknowledge that he has witnessed the sealing of their union.

If you are a Jewish–Greek Orthodox couple, you may wish to consider including the crowning in your ceremony.

The Agape Meal

This is a ritual of sharing bread and wine as part of the wedding ceremony. Over the centuries, numerous religious communities have included bread and wine as part of their traditional meals. During the first century, Christians began the tradition of agape meals, or love feasts, to build community and to feed souls. Such a meal is sometimes included in a wedding ceremony to honor the love the couple shares and to express their hopes and our hopes that they will build a community of love around them.[1]

Announcing the Bride and Groom as Mr. and Mrs. (Blank)
at the End of the Ceremony

Some priests and ministers introduce the bride and groom for the first time with their married name. At the end of the ceremony, immediately before the recessional begins, the officiant says:

Now, for the first time, as husband and wife, I introduce you to Mr. and Mrs. (Ms.) _____.

This particular custom seems to be getting less popular. Only a few couples I have married have requested this.

Choosing Customs for Your Ceremony

In this and the previous section, I have explained some Jewish and Christian customs that you may wish to include in your own ceremony. Of course, this list is not complete. You may know of other customs you would like to use, or you may wish to give new meaning to some old traditions.

One couple I married, for example, liked the idea of the seven wedding blessings, but they did not feel connected to the content of the traditional Hebrew blessings and they felt that the traditional blessings placed too much emphasis on the Jewish part of the ceremony. As an alternative, they asked seven people, representing seven different cultures and religions, to give them a blessing from their own heritages. The result was a wonderful set of blessings from Jewish, Christian, Irish, Russian, Italian, Chinese, and Native American heritages that celebrated the diversity of their family and friends as well as their own love and relationship. These blessings are included in the section on "The Seven Jewish Wedding Blessings" in Part III.

Another couple I know felt very uncomfortable about changing any aspect of their families' traditions and customs. For this Jewish-Episcopal couple, it was important to select an equal number of traditional passages and customs from each side. This ceremony and the innovative ceremony I mentioned above were very different, but, in my eyes, they were equally beautiful because the guests and I could see and feel how much these couples believed in what they were saying and doing.

As you consider various options for your service, let your heart be your guide. Select, add, and adapt passages and customs that appeal to you and those that help you and your families feel connected to your different traditions. This is the key to making your wedding ceremony a very meaningful and moving beginning to your marriage.

When Jewish and
Christian Traditions Conflict

Jewish and Christian wedding ceremonies and customs complement each other very well, but there are places where they can conflict. It is an American Christian tradition, for example, for the bride not to see her groom before the ceremony. It is considered bad luck for her to see him before the processional begins. But it is a common Jewish practice for the bride and groom to see each other before the ceremony, when they sign their ketubah. If you want to sign a ketubah and you do not want to see each other before the ceremony, you have a conflict. What can you do? Is there any way to resolve this conflict without giving up one custom or the other? The answer is yes! In this chapter I will present you with at least one solution to this and other common conflicts that exist between Jewish and Christian wedding customs and practices.

The Time of the Wedding

Many Christian couples prefer to be married on a Saturday afternoon, but this time is not an option for Jewish couples. According to Jewish tradition, weddings are not held on the Sabbath, which technically begins at sundown on Friday and ends at sundown on Saturday. Consequently, most interfaith weddings are scheduled for a Saturday evening or Sunday.

If you want a Saturday evening wedding, talk to your rabbi about the starting time. Many rabbis will agree to officiate at a 6:00 P.M. June wedding, for example, even though the sun does not set until much later. This is possible because rabbis are free to determine for themselves when they feel it is appropriate to begin a Saturday service.

The Date of the Wedding

While Christian weddings may be held on any day of the year, Jewish weddings cannot. According to Jewish practice, weddings are not performed on certain holidays. These include Rosh Hashanah, Yom Kippur, and Sukkot, which occur in the fall, and Passover, which occurs sometime in the spring, around Easter, as well as other days. The exact dates of these holidays vary from year to year relative to the Gregorian calendar because the Jewish calendar differs from our secular, solar calendar. The Jewish calendar is determined by a combination of lunar and solar cycles. To avoid conflicts, check the Jewish calendar and talk with your rabbi before you set your date.

The Location of the Wedding

Most synagogues will not permit interfaith ceremonies to be held in their sanctuaries. Catholic, Protestant, and Unitarian churches will welcome you, but most rabbis will not participate in a wedding that takes place in a church setting. Perhaps this is for the best. A church or synagogue wedding would delight one side of the family but no doubt make the other side uncomfortable. For these reasons, most interfaith ceremonies take place in neutral settings, such as nondenominational chapels, historical sites, public gardens, hotels, and private homes.

To See or Not to See Each Other
Before the Ceremony

As mentioned earlier, many brides do not want to see their groom before the processional begins because they believe this would bring them bad luck. What do you do if you want to sign an interfaith ketubah but you do not want to see each other before the ceremony?

You do have a couple of options. If your rabbi or officiant is willing, you can sign the ketubah immediately following the ceremony, but I discourage this practice. After the ceremony, you will be anxious to take pictures and to see your family and friends, so the signing is often rushed. I have found that the ritual of signing the ketubah is much more powerful and meaningful to the couple when they sign it, calmly and thoughtfully, before the service. There is another solution, a way you can sign your ketubah before the ceremony without seeing each other. Your rabbi or officiant can have you sign your ketubah separately before the music begins. First, he or she could take the ketubah to the bride and her witness(es) for their signatures and then take the document to the groom and his witness(es) for their signatures. This option allows you to keep the power and significance of the ketubah signing and the good luck of not seeing each other before the ceremony begins.

The Processional

There are no hard-and-fast rules regarding processionals, but each tradition has developed its own particular customs. It is a Jewish tradition, for example, for the parents of both the bride and groom to walk their children down the aisle; and it is a Christian custom for the groom to walk in alone and for the bride to be escorted by her father. Here are outlines of (1) a typical Jewish processional, (2) a typical Christian processional, and (3) a popular alternative that combines some Jewish and Christian elements.

TYPICAL JEWISH PROCESSIONAL

Rabbi enters from the side and takes his/her place under the huppah. If the huppah is handheld, the huppah holders enter first. They may carry the huppah with them or pick it up near the site of the ceremony.

Groom's grandparents walk down the aisle and sit in seats reserved for them in the front row. If a grandparent is a widow or widower, he or she is escorted down the aisle by an usher or by a designated family member.

Bride's grandparents walk down the aisle and sit in seats reserved for them in the front row. As mentioned above, when a grandparent is a widow or widower, he or she is escorted down the aisle by an usher or by a designated family member.

Ushers
Best man
Groom's father, groom, groom's mother
Attendants (bridesmaids)
Best woman (maid of honor)
Bride's father, bride, bride's mother

The bride stands to the right of the groom.

STANDARD AMERICAN AND CHRISTIAN PROCESSIONAL

The groom and best man walk in from the side with the minister or priest.

Groom's grandparents walk down the aisle and take their place in seats reserved for them in the front row. If a grandparent is a widow or widower, he or she is escorted by an usher or designated family member.

Bride's grandparents walk down the aisle and take their places in seats reserved for them in the first row. If a grandparent is a widow or widower, he or she is escorted down the aisle by an usher or designated family member.

Bride's mother is escorted to her seat.
Groom's parents take their seats.
Ushers
Attendants (bridesmaids)
Best woman (maid of honor)
Flower girl and ring bearer
Bride escorted by her father

The bride stands to the left of the groom.

ALTERNATIVE PROCESSIONAL

Rabbi, priest, and/or minister enters from the side.

Groom's grandparents walk down the aisle and take the seats reserved for them in the front row. If a grandparent is a widow or widower, he or she is escorted down the aisle by an usher or designated family member.

Bride's grandparents walk down the aisle and take seats reserved for them in the front row. If a grandparent is a widow or widower, he or she is escorted down the aisle by an usher or by a designated family member.

Groom's parents
Ushers
Best man
Groom
Attendants (bridesmaids)
Best woman (maid or matron of honor)
Bride's parents walk halfway down the aisle and stop.

The bride walks in alone until she meets her parents. Then the three of them walk together up to the huppah or wedding site. The bride's parents give her a kiss and take their places. The bride and groom walk under the huppah or to the wedding site.

or

The bride walks in with both her parents. They stop halfway down the aisle. The bride's parents give her a kiss; then the bride walks alone to meet the groom. The parents take their seats, and the bride and groom walk under the huppah or to the wedding site.

This order, or a variation of it, symbolizes the bride's independence. She chooses to marry; her parents do not "give her away."

The order that is right for you will depend on your own feelings, your family traditions, and your family circumstances. One couple I married broke from tradition and invited the groom's only living grandmother to escort him down the aisle. The guests and I were very moved. In another case, one set of parents was divorced and not on good terms with each other, so the bride and groom decided to simplify the processional by having their parents seated before the formal processional began. Again, there are no rules about processionals. Choose an order that considers your family's and your own feelings.

Where Does the Wedding Party Stand?

In the Jewish tradition, the bride stands on the right side of the groom. It is a Christian tradition for the bride to stand on his left. The rest of the wedding party stands to either side of the couple. When there is a large wedding party I recommend that everyone stand in a **V** shape, fanning out from the huppah or wedding space. The following diagram illustrates this format; the poles of a huppah are represented by the asterisks. The parents, standing between the poles, are indicated by the plus signs.

		*		*	
Best man	+	Rabbi/Minister	+	Best woman	
Usher	+	Groom and Bride	+	Bridesmaid	
Usher				Bridesmaid	
Usher	*		*	Bridesmaid	
		Guests			

This format allows everyone to witness the ceremony without blocking anyone's view.

In summary, the basic conflicts between Jewish and Christian processionals are as follows: (1) In the Jewish tradition the bride stands on the right side of the groom; it is the reverse in the Christian tradition. (2) In the Jewish tradition, the groom walks down the aisle with both of his parents and the bride walks down with both of her parents. In the Christian tradition, the groom's parents and the bride's mother are escorted to their seats before the formal processional begins, and the bride's father escorts her down the aisle. (3) In the Jewish tradition, the parents stand near the bride and groom for the entire ceremony. In Christian tradition, the parents are seated for the service.

The right processional for you will be the one that meets your needs and special circumstances. If you are the bride and your father has always dreamed of walking you down the aisle, and if you have no strong objections to this yourself, then you, no doubt, will choose to make his dream come true. But sometimes these choices are complicated when each side of the family wants something different. What if your Jewish parents feel very strongly about standing with you during the ceremony and your Christian partner's parents want to remain seated? It would be awkward for one set of parents to stand and the other to sit. If you run into one of these conflicts, you can only do your best. Talk it out carefully between the two of you first, and then decide what you want for yourselves. In most cases, your parents will follow your wishes. If you cannot resolve a conflict, try to compromise, keeping your own priorities in mind. This is your big day, after all!

Processional Music

Many brides dream of walking down the aisle to "Here Comes the Bride"—their wedding would not be the same without it. But this piece, written by Wagner, is usually avoided in Jewish weddings because it is widely known that Wagner was anti-Semitic. If you really want to use "Here Comes the Bride," talk to your rabbi and to your families. Sometimes everyone involved will feel comfortable including this piece, even with the history behind it.

A few rabbis also have an issue with Mendelssohn's wedding march from his *Midsummer Night's Dream*. If you would like to include this piece in your ceremony, first talk to him or her.

If you need or want help choosing music, talk to any musician who performs at both Jewish and Christian weddings. He/she will provide you with a wide variety of selections. You can also hear a sampling of wedding music on the Internet. Simply search for wedding music and you will find several audiofiles.

Music can enhance any ceremony, if the pieces are not too numerous or too long. If you want to include music in your service, I suggest that you add only two or three pieces. If you include more, you will break the flow of your ceremony.

Where do you insert the music? Anywhere you like, but there are a few places that naturally call for some music. They are the lighting of the unity candle and the silent prayers. Most couples like some soft instrumentals playing in the background during these pauses in speaking and reading. If you include more than one piece of music in your service, try to distribute them evenly throughout the ceremony. This will help keep your service balanced yet varied. See the sample ceremonies in Part II for more ideas about the placement of music in your service.

Do Guests Stand or Sit as the Bride Enters?

It is an American Christian tradition for the guests to rise as the bride enters, and it is a Jewish custom for everyone to remain seated throughout the processional and the ceremony. If you do not tell your guests whether to stand or sit, some will stand and others will remain seated as the bride makes her appearance. This can be an awkward, uncomfortable moment for everyone. To avoid confusion, inform your officiant what you want your guests to do. He or she can then instruct your guests to rise or remain seated as the bride begins her walk down the aisle.

The Rehearsal

Although most priests and ministers attend rehearsals, most rabbis do not. There is no religious reason why this difference exists; it simply reflects different practices. Yet all clergy agree that a rehearsal is important. It helps everyone feel less anxious and it is added insurance that the wedding will run smoothly. Rehearsals generally focus on the processional and recessional and on the positioning of any readers that may be included in the service. Few rehearsals include a reading of the service itself.

If your clergy or officiant cannot be present at the rehearsal, ask your wedding or event coordinator or a friend to lead the rehearsal and to help direct you on your wedding day.

Programs

Programs, in their most basic form, are small pamphlets that give guests an outline of the service, including the names of the participants. Programs are not generally a part of Jewish ceremonies, but they are frequently a part of Christian and interfaith weddings. In addition to providing a outline of your service, a program can help your guests understand and appreciate your ceremony by including some explanations of the elements and customs in your ceremony.

Some couples carry the program to an extreme by including the entire text of their ceremony. I strongly discourage this path because guests who have the text in their hands are more likely to read rather than listen to the ceremony, and a wedding is designed to be heard and watched.

The Use of Hebrew

Some Hebrew is usually included in interfaith ceremonies, even though many of the Jewish guests and most of the non-Jewish guests cannot speak or read the language. Why? Because for most Jews a service without any Hebrew feels strange. Hebrew is the language of the Bible and the Jewish prayer book. Its familiar sounds and rhythms link Jews to their ancestors and their heritage in ways that English cannot. To help everyone feel included, I suggest that you add translations or paraphrases for any Hebrew you use.

How much Hebrew you should include in your service will depend on your own needs and tastes, but most couples include at least the Hebrew blessing over the wine and the Hebrew for the Priestly Benediction at the end of the ceremony. You may also wish to include the Hebrew of the seven Jewish wedding blessings (see "The Seven Jewish Wedding Blessings" in Part III). Some couples worry that including this much Hebrew will make the service too long, but this is not true. Reciting all the Hebrew listed above takes no more than five minutes.

If you do decide to include the Hebrew of the seven blessings, I suggest that you alternate reciting the Hebrew and English of each. Reciting all seven in Hebrew, without a break, will make your guests a little sleepy unless, of course, they all understand the language.

Who Wears Yarmulkes?

Jewish men and some Jewish women wear yarmulkes, or skullcaps, at religious ceremonies as a sign of respect for God. But what about the non-Jewish guests? Are they required to wear yarmulkes if they are provided? The answer is no. When we go to a church or synagogue, we follow the customs of the place we are visiting. During an interfaith wedding, we are usually on neutral ground, at a hotel, home, or historical site. In this case, we each represent ourselves. If you are providing yarmulkes for your Jewish guests, I recommend that you put an OPTIONAL sign over the basket that holds them. In this way, Jewish men and women can wear one if they wish, and the non-Jewish men know they are not obligated to do so.

Not every interfaith wedding requires yarmulkes. Sometimes the Jewish side does not have a history of wearing them, so check with your families to determine whether or not you should provide them.

To purchase yarmulkes, call your nearest Jewish gift shop or bookstore for prices and selections. And remember that you do not need to buy one for every guest.

Non-Jewish grooms often ask me if they should wear a yarmulke out of respect for their partner's family and heritage. This is a very kind gesture, and it is fine if he wants to wear one, but it is not necessary.

If you have ordered dozens of yarmulkes for your wedding, what will you do with them after the wedding? Most couples keep a handful or more for their new family, but very few couples will need as many as they use on their wedding day. Consider donating your extras to a local synagogue or Jewish organization or to your rabbi, who will distribute them to those in need. Even if you have your names printed on the inside of the caps, these donations are welcome.

Blessing Before the Meal

It is a Jewish custom for a family member, often a grandparent, to say the Hebrew blessing over the bread before the meal that follows the wedding ceremony. The blessing is:

בָּרוּךְ אַתָּה יְיָ אֱלֹהֵינוּ מֶלֶךְ הָעוֹלָם הַמוֹצִיא לֶחֶם מִן הָאָרֶץ.

Blessed are you, O God, Who brings forth bread from the earth.

If you use this traditional Hebrew prayer, remember to recite the English translation as well. The use of any Hebrew without the translation will feel alienating to non-Jewish guests.

Many priests and ministers offer an extemporaneous grace before the meal that includes a prayer for the bride and groom and all the guests, as well as some form of the following blessing:

> O God, bless this food which we are about to receive, and make us ever mindful of the needs of others.

For interfaith weddings, you might consider asking a representative from each side of the family to offer a blessing.

Final Touches:
Details That Make a Difference

There are so many details to consider when planning a wedding that it is easy to miss some important odds and ends, such as insect repellent for outdoor weddings, microphones for the officiants and readers, and important instructions for the photographer and videographer. One couple I married arranged to exchange their vows and rings on the top deck of a harbor cruise ship. The setting was beautiful, but the wind was strong, as it often is on the ocean. Neither of them thought about using a microphone; yet, if we had not arranged for the mike, no one would have heard the words of the ceremony that they worked so hard to craft.

Seating Arrangements

Most couples seat their guests in straight rows in front of the huppah, altar, or area in which the ceremony takes place. Although this arrangement is a bit formal, it is practical. The rows allow everyone to see and hear the ceremony, assuming the officiant is using a microphone or projecting his/her voice.

Some couples like to arrange the seating in a semicircle because it feels more informal and more intimate than the standard rows. However, those guests seated toward the sides may not be able to see the wedding party very well and they may not be able to hear the service clearly, especially if the wedding is held outside and/or the officiant is not using a microphone.

Some couples also consider asking their guests to stand for the service.

I discourage this unless the guest list is very small. In a larger group, some guests will inevitably find themselves behind a taller person, unable to see the bride and groom. Also, seating the guests adds a sense of importance to the event. When seated, everyone can pay more attention to the ceremony.

If you must ask your guests to stand because of your space or circumstances, ask everyone to move up close to you, and have a few chairs available for frail elderly, the ill, and/or handicapped.

Microphones

For most weddings, a microphone is a must. Unless your wedding is very small, or unless you are holding your service in a hall with great acoustics, I strongly recommend that you use a microphone. Even if your officiant projects his/her voice, you will still need a mike if you want your guests to hear your exchange of vows. The microphone also allows each participant to use his/her natural speaking voice, a voice that is usually warmer and more expressive than a voice that is straining to be heard.

Many couples hesitate to use a microphone because they do not want their very intimate ceremony booming through loudspeakers. That would be disturbing, but if the volume of the system is set properly, you will not hear any reverberation; you will not even notice the amplification.

For most ceremonies, one freestanding mike should be sufficient. The mike will face your officiant(s) for most of the service. Then, when it is time to exchange your vows, he or she can turn the microphone toward you. If you have one or two additional readers, they can also use this mike. They can simply come up to the mike where it stands, or your officiant can take the mike off the stand and hand it to them. If you are having a large wedding and plan to include several speakers, I advise using two microphones, one for you and your officiant(s) and one for your readers. If you are using a readers' mike, I suggest placing it about six to twelve feet to either side of the ceremony site. This will allow your readers easy access to the mike and it will permit you and your guests to watch the readers as they speak.

Lapel mikes also work well, but if you use these, you will need one for each officiant. These mikes are very sensitive, so they will also pick up your voices when you exchange your vows, assuming that your officiant is facing you and standing relatively close to you.

I strongly discourage the use of handheld mikes. It is very difficult for readers to hold a mike and read from a paper at the same time, and these mikes will pick up all sorts of extraneous sounds. I also do not recommend podium mikes. They are cumbersome and create an awkward barrier between you and your officiant.

If you have hired musicians, you may be able to use one of their microphones for your service. If not, you can rent mikes. If you are having an outdoor wedding, remember to check the placement of the electrical outlets. You may need to bring or rent a long extension cord. There are also portable, battery-powered mikes that do not require any electrical hookups, but they are often not available for rent.

Remember, always test your sound system before your ceremony begins!

Placement of the Ritual Items

You will need a *small* table for any ritual items you will use in your ceremony. These items may include two wine cups, a glass to break, candles, and your wedding rings. Which items you need will depend on the content of your service.

Your natural inclination will be to place the table in the center of the huppah or space you will be using. The table does look good here, but it is not the best place for it. If you place the table in the center, it will stand between you and your officiant, creating an awkward barrier. Also keep in mind that if the table is too large, it will prevent you from standing totally under the huppah, should you be using one.

If you are not lighting candles, I recommend that you place the table toward the back of the ceremony area, the table out of your way but still within easy reach of your officiant(s). If you are lighting candles as a part of your service, place the table toward the front and to the side of the area in which you will stand:

Clergy

Bride and Groom

Table

With the table here, you will be able to light the candles easily, and your guests will be able to enjoy the beauty of the flames throughout your ceremony. Your officiant(s) also has easy access to the other items, such as the cup of wine that he or she will handle during the service.

Outdoor Wedding Preparations

Outdoor weddings are beautiful, but they require some special attention. Remember that any wind will prevent you from lighting candles, and the same wind will make it very difficult for your guests to hear the words of your service unless you are using a microphone.

With all outdoor weddings, it is important to have alternative plans if it should rain on your wedding day. Tents or adjacent indoor rooms are the most common choices for backups.

Also remember that the earth can be very soft and unfriendly to women wearing high heels. If you are planning to have your ceremony on the bare ground, alert your guests. Encourage the women to wear low-heeled shoes.

In the summer, insects can make you and your guests very uncomfortable. Even if the area is sprayed before the ceremony, it may still not be pest-free. Make sure you have some type of insect repellent available for everyone.

Photography

Most officiants allow pictures to be taken during the ceremony, but some do not. Be sure to check with your rabbi, priest, or minister about his/her policy.

While most photographers are discreet when taking pictures, some are not. Talk to your photographer about his/her plans before the ceremony. I strongly urge you not to allow any photographer—professionals, family members, or friends—to position themselves around you or behind you during the ceremony. This will distract you and detract from the ceremony.

Sometimes several guests want to take their own pictures. It is wonderful that they want to be so involved, but their involvement can disrupt your service with flashing lights and the constant sound of clicking and the whir of winding film. Guest photographers can also interfere with the professional photographer's work. Because of these potential problems, you may wish to consider asking your guests to refrain from taking pictures during your ceremony. If you like, you can offer to send them copies of pictures taken by the professional.

Videography

If you want to videotape your ceremony, check with your clergy first. Some officiants will not allow it.

When videographers are present, they should film from a stationary position near the couple and officiant(s). This seems to work well.

Participation of Family and Friends

Participation of family and friends can add a warm, personal touch to your ceremony. There are many different ways to include them. You may ask them to (1) be a member of the wedding party; (2) read a part of the service; (3) be a huppah holder; (4) play some music; (5) sing a song; or (6) join with the other guests in song or readings.

If you are planning to create a participatory ceremony, remember to ask everyone, in advance, if they are willing to participate, and keep the number of participants small. Too many speakers will interrupt the flow of the service. How many are too many depends on the length and type of your ceremony and the placement of the readers. If, for example, you want every reader to come forward and read with a microphone and then sit down, I recommend that you limit the number of participants to three or four. The movement of more individuals up and down the aisles disrupts the service. You may, however, include a larger number of people if you have each read from his or her place. It is not uncommon, for example, for seven people to stand at their seats and read the traditional seven wedding blessings in a Jewish ceremony. This format can work well if the participants project their voices. If you have any soft-spoken readers, however, you and your guests may not hear their words, especially if you are outdoors and/or have a large number of guests. Before you decide to ask people to read from their seats, consider the size of your gathering, the strength of your speakers' voices, the acoustics of your space, and the positioning of your guests. If you do choose to have several speakers, ask them to sit near the outside edges of your seating area. When they stand and read, they will then be facing most of your guests. Remember, anyone sitting behind your readers will have a hard time hearing their words.

Honoring Parents

There are many ways to honor your parents on your wedding day. You might (1) ask them to stand with you during your ceremony; (2) present them with a flower as a symbol of your love and appreciation; (3) share one of the cups of wine with them; (4) ask them to participate in the unity candle ritual. Your mothers can light the two smaller candles at the beginning of the wedding ceremony. By doing so, they are symbolizing their role in raising you and helping you become the individuals you are (see "The Unity Candle" in Part III for a more detailed explanation of this ritual). And, finally, you might include your parents by (5) asking them to acknowledge their support of your marriage as part of the wedding ceremony (see "Affirmations of the Family and of the Guests" in Part III).

Including Children from a Previous Marriage

If you already have children, you may wish to include them in your service. Smaller children can serve as ring bearers and flower girls. They can help you light a candle, or they may simply stand with you during the ceremony. Older children can recite an appropriate passage or special reading; or you may wish to include them in your wedding party.

In all cases, I think it is important to acknowledge your love for your children during the service. Your rabbi and/or priest or minister can do this for you in his or her remarks, or you may want to say something directly to them. During one ceremony I witnessed, the father gave his young daughter a necklace as a sign of his continuing love for her. Small but powerful touches assure your children that your new partner will not diminish your love for them.

Checklist of Items to Bring to Your Wedding

You will need to bring some, if not all, of the following items:

1. Marriage license
2. Wedding rings
3. Huppah (wedding canopy)
4. Yarmulkes (if you need them); bobby pins to hold the yarmulkes in place
5. Kiddush cup, or wine goblet
6. Wine (preferably on the sweet side, to symbolize the sweetness and richness of your life together)
7. Glass to break. This is not usually the kiddush cup, but a separate glass. I recommend using an inexpensive, stemmed wine glass.
8. Napkin or cloth in which to wrap the glass you will break. The covering protects your foot.
9. Small table for the ritual items, e.g., kiddush cup, wine, candles
10 Ketubah, or marriage contract or covenant, if you have one
11. A black pen to use for signing the ketubah and license
12. Candles, candlesticks, and matches if you are including a candle-lighting ceremony in your service
13. Microphone if you need one (see "Microphones")
14. Copies of your vows and/or readings for you and participants (if applicable)
15. Copy of your ceremony, for any last-minute changes.

Creating Your Own Interfaith Service: From the First Draft to the Final Version

After reviewing the basics of wedding ceremonies in Part I, you are ready to create your own ceremony. Simply follow these easy steps, and you will have a ceremony that is moving and meaningful to you and to your guests.

Step 1: Read All of the Sample Services

First, read all the sample ceremonies in Part II, even if the titles do not apply to you. These services were selected not only for their different religious combinations, but also for their different styles. You may find parts in each that you would like to include in your own service. By reading all of these ceremonies, you will also learn, very quickly, about the basic elements and flow of a wedding service.

You may discover that you like one of these ceremonies so much that you want to use it as the basic outline for your own service. If you are not happy with any of the sample ceremonies, do not worry; simply move on to step 2.

Step 2: Choose Passages for Your Ceremony

Turn to Part III, "Menu of Passages for Each Element of the Service." Simply choose one passage from each element that you wish to include in your service. If you place your selections in the order in which they appear in this guide, you will have the first draft of your ceremony.

Step 3: Edit Your First Draft

Check to see if you like the order and flow of your first draft. Remember, there are no absolute rules about the order of a ceremony. Some couples like to build up to their exchange of vows and rings, and then end quickly with the pronouncement, benediction, and breaking of the glass. Others prefer to place their exchange of vows and rings toward the middle of the ceremony, with blessings and readings on either side. Which style you prefer will depend on your personal taste.

Insert extra readings from Part IV or from your own resources. You can place your readings anywhere you like throughout your service, but, generally, New Testament and Torah, or Hebrew Scripture, readings are inserted toward the beginning of the ceremony. Ideally, biblical and secular poetry and prose should be placed where their content naturally flows from the preceding passage of the service, but this is not always possible. Review the sample ceremonies for ideas on the placement of readings. Also, ask your officiant for guidance and for help with transitions that may seem awkward.

Edit the passages you have chosen. You may need to change a word or two to make the passages reflect your own style, thoughts, and feelings.

Step 4: Review Your Draft with Your Officiant

Review your first draft with your officiant(s), making whatever changes you need to enhance your ceremony and help each of you feel comfortable with the text.

Step 5: The Final Touches

Now you are ready to decide who will read the various parts of your service. In most ceremonies, the officiant leads the service; the bride and groom speak only when they exchange their vows and rings; and family members or friends often read the special biblical and secular poetry and prose.

When a ceremony is co-officiated, the rabbi usually leads the uniquely

Jewish elements and the priest or minister leads the Christian elements. Any remaining passages are divided equally between the two.

Step 6: Enjoy Your Creation

You have now written the final version of your own, personalized wedding ceremony!

· PART II ·

Sample Ceremonies

Two Jewish-style Ceremonies

A Jewish-style ceremony is a service that includes few, if any, Christian customs or passages. All the basic elements of a Jewish ceremony are present, with the exception of those words and passages that imply that both the bride and groom are Jewish.

General Jewish-style Ceremony
Officiated by a Rabbi

(Time: approximately 25 minutes)

1. Opening Remarks
2. Acknowledging Loved Ones Who Have Died
3. Opening Blessing of the Couple
4. Explanation of the Huppah
5. General Blessing: *Shehecheyanu*
6. Rabbi's Remarks
7. Blessing over the Wine
8. Exchange of Vows
9. Exchange of Rings
10. Candle Lighting
11. Seven Wedding Blessings
12. Pronouncement
13. Benediction

14. Explanation of the Yichud
15. Breaking of the Glass

*[The mothers of the bride and groom, or partners,
each light one of two small candles.]*

OPENING REMARKS

Rabbi:
Welcome family and friends. (Bride) and (groom) are happy that so many of you who mean so much to them are here to celebrate their wedding this day. Your role here is not a passive one; you are encouraged not only to rejoice and honor the bride and groom on their wedding day, but also to remain a sustaining community for them.

ACKNOWLEDGING LOVED ONES WHO HAVE DIED

Rabbi:
There are also those who were close to (bride) and (groom) who are no longer with us but who we remember today, because they have been such an important part of their lives. Their spirits touched them and helped make them the individuals they are. Let us remember them now in a moment of silence.

OPENING BLESSING

Rabbi:
(Bride) and (groom), I bless you with these traditional Hebrew words along with an English interpretation.

בְּרוּכִים הַבָּאִים בְּשֵׁם יְיָ.

Blessed be you who have come here in dedication to all that is loving, good, and sacred.

עִבְדוּ אֶת יְיָ בְּשִׂמְחָה. בֹּאוּ לְפָנָיו בִּרְנָנָה.

We bless you and welcome you in joy.

מִי אַדִּיר עַל הַכֹּל. מִי בָּרוּךְ עַל הַכֹּל. מִי גָּדוֹל עַל הַכֹּל. הוּא
יְבָרֵךְ אֶת-הֶחָתָן וְאֶת-הַכַּלָּה.

May the Source of life sustain you in life.
May all that is noble and true in the universe
Inspire your lives together and
Bring peace to all humankind.[1]

EXPLANATION OF THE HUPPAH

Rabbi:
Surrounded by loved ones whose joy and prayers are with you, you stand
at this huppah, a symbol of your new home. Its four sides are open, symbolizing the importance of community and of participation in each
other's lives. Friends and family fill the home. May your home be a shelter against the storms, a haven of peace, a stronghold of faith and love.

GENERAL BLESSING: SHEHECHEYANU

Rabbi:

בָּרוּךְ אַתָּה יְיָ אֱלוֹהֵינוּ מֶלֶךְ הָעוֹלָם שֶׁהֶחֱיָנוּ וְקִיְּמָנוּ וְהִגִּיעָנוּ
לַזְּמַן הַזֶּה.

Blessed are you, O God, for giving us life, for sustaining us,
and bringing us to this joyous time.

RABBI'S REMARKS
The rabbi's personal remarks to the bride and groom.

BLESSING OVER THE WINE

Rabbi:
This cup of wine represents the cup of life. As you share this cup of wine,
you undertake to share all that the future may bring. All of the sweetness

life's cup may hold for you will be sweeter because you drink it together. Whatever drops of bitterness it may contain will be less bitter because you share them.[2]

בָּרוּךְ אַתָּה יְיָ אֱלֹהֵינוּ מֶלֶךְ הָעוֹלָם בּוֹרֵא פְּרִי הַגָּפֶן.

Blessed are you, our God, Ruler of the universe, Creator of the fruit of the vine.

EXCHANGE OF VOWS

Rabbi:
And now your vows to one another:
   Do you, (bride), take (groom) to be your husband, to have and to hold, to love and to cherish, to honor and respect, forsaking all others? Do you promise to love him, in sickness and health, for richer or poorer, for better or worse, for now and forever?

Bride:
I do.

Rabbi:
Do you, (groom), take (bride) to be your wife, to have and to hold, to love and to cherish, to honor and respect, forsaking all others? Do you promise to love her, in sickness and health, for richer or poorer, for better or worse, for now and forever?

Groom:
I do.

EXCHANGE OF RINGS

Rabbi:
These rings in their unbroken wholeness are tokens of your union and your love. They are symbols of the enduring trust and affection that you bring one another.

(Groom), as you place the ring on (bride)'s finger, repeat after me: By this ring, you are consecrated (or sanctified) to me as my wife.

(Bride), as you place the ring on (groom)'s finger, repeat after me: By this ring, you are consecrated (or sanctified) to me as my husband.

CANDLE LIGHTING

> *[Bride and groom each take one of the small*
> *candles and light one larger candle.]*

Rabbi:
From every human being there rises a light that reaches straight to heaven. And when two souls are destined to find one another, their two streams of light flow together and a single brighter light goes forth from their united being.

(Baal Shem Tov)

SEVEN WEDDING BLESSINGS

Rabbi:
In the Jewish tradition, brides and grooms are blessed with seven wedding blessings. Six of these blessings thank God for creating the world, man and woman, peace and harmony, and the joy of the bride and groom. The seventh, the blessing over the wine, symbolically sanctifies this day and this marriage.

(Bride) and (groom), I now bless you with these traditional Hebrew blessings, along with an English interpretation of them.

בָּרוּךְ אַתָּה יְיָ אֱלוֹהֵינוּ מֶלֶךְ הָעוֹלָם שֶׁהַכֹּל בָּרָא לִכְבוֹדוֹ.

We acknowledge the Unity of all, realizing that each separate moment and every distinct object points to and shares in this oneness.

בָּרוּךְ אַתָּה יְיָ אֱלוֹהֵינוּ מֶלֶךְ הָעוֹלָם יוֹצֵר הָאָדָם.

We acknowledge the Unity of all, recognizing and appreciating the blessing of being human.

בָּרוּךְ אַתָּה יְיָ אֱלֹהֵינוּ מֶלֶךְ הָעוֹלָם, אֲשֶׁר יָצַר אֶת-הָאָדָם בְּצַלְמוֹ, בְּצֶלֶם דְּמוּת תַּבְנִיתוֹ, וְהִתְקִין לוֹ מִמֶּנּוּ בִּנְיַן עֲדֵי עַד. בָּרוּךְ אַתָּה יְיָ יוֹצֵר הָאָדָם.

We acknowledge the Unity of all, realizing the special gift of awareness that permits us the perceive this unity, and the wonder we experience as a man and a woman joined together to live as one.

שׂוֹשׂ תָּשִׂישׂ וְתָגֵל צִיּוֹן בְּקִבּוּץ בָּנֶיהָ לְתוֹכָהּ בְּשִׂמְחָה. בָּרוּךְ אַתָּה יְיָ מְשַׂמֵּחַ צִיּוֹן בְּבָנֶיהָ.

May rejoicing resound throughout the world as the homeless are given homes, persecution and oppression cease, and all people learn to live in peace with each other and in harmony with their environment.

שַׂמֵּחַ תְּשַׂמַּח רֵעִים הָאֲהוּבִים כְּשַׂמֵּחֲךָ יְצִירְךָ בְּגַן עֵדֶן מִקֶּדֶם. בָּרוּךְ אַתָּה יְיָ מְשַׂמֵּחַ חָתָן וְכַלָּה.

From the Source of all energy we call forth an abundance of love to envelop this couple. May they be for each other lovers and friends, and may their love partake of the same innocence, purity, and sense of discovery that we imagine the first couple to have experienced.

בָּרוּךְ אַתָּה יְיָ אֱלֹהֵינוּ מֶלֶךְ הָעוֹלָם, אֲשֶׁר בָּרָא שָׂשׂוֹן וְשִׂמְחָה, חָתָן וְכַלָּה, גִּילָה, רִנָּה, דִּיצָה וְחֶדְוָה, אַהֲבָה וְאַחֲוָה, שָׁלוֹם וְרֵעוּת. מְהֵרָה יְיָ אֱלֹהֵינוּ יִשָּׁמַע בְּעָרֵי יְהוּדָה וּבְחוּצוֹת יְרוּשָׁלַיִם, קוֹל שָׂשׂוֹן וְקוֹל שִׂמְחָה, קוֹל חָתָן וְקוֹל כַּלָּה, קוֹל מִצְהֲלוֹת חֲתָנִים מֵחֻפָּתָם וּנְעָרִים מִמִּשְׁתֵּה נְגִינָתָם. בָּרוּךְ אַתָּה יְיָ מְשַׂמֵּחַ חָתָן עִם-הַכַּלָּה.

We acknowledge the Unity of all, and we highlight today joy and gladness, bridegroom and bride, delight and cheer, love and harmony, peace and companionship. May we all witness the day when the dominant sounds in Jerusalem and throughout the world will be these sounds of happiness, the voices of lovers, the sounds of feasting and singing. Praised is love; blessed be this marriage. May the bride and bridegroom rejoice together.

בָּרוּךְ אַתָּה יְיָ אֱלוֹהֵינוּ מֶלֶךְ הָעוֹלָם בּוֹרֵא פְּרִי הַגָּפֶן.

We acknowledge the Unity of all, expressing our appreciation for this wine, symbol of our rejoicing.[3]

PRONOUNCEMENT

Rabbi:
Your friends and family, all of us here, rejoice in your happiness and we pray that this day marks only one of many more blessings you will share in the days and years ahead. And now that you have spoken the words and performed the rites that unite your lives, we now, by the power of your love and the commitment you have made, declare your marriage to be valid and binding, and declare you, (groom) and (bride), husband and wife.

[Bride and groom kiss.]

BENEDICTION

    Rabbi:

יִהְיֶה דַרְכְּךָ מְבוֹרָךְ.

May your way be blessed.

יָאֵר אֵלֶיךָ אוֹר הַחָכְמָה.

May wisdom's light shine upon you.

יָבִיאוּ לְךָ מָסַעֲךָ שָׁלוֹם.

May your journey bring you peace.

THE YICHUD

Rabbi:

I would like to take this opportunity to mention to you, the guests, that (bride) and (groom) will be spending a few moments alone together, immediately following the ceremony. This is a custom called Yichud, which means union, in Hebrew. It gives the couple an opportunity to share, privately, the power and importance of this moment in their lives. They will return shortly to greet you.

BREAKING OF THE GLASS

Rabbi:

The traditional breaking of the glass marks the end of the ceremony and the beginning of the celebration.

As (groom) breaks the glass, I invite everyone to shout "Mazel Tov," which means "Congratulations" and "Good Luck."

[Bride and groom kiss.]

The Wedding Ceremony of
Linda Graetz and Jim Eng

(Time: approximately 35 minutes)

This service contains most of the same elements that are found in the previous Jewish-style ceremony, but here the couple add their unique touch.

1. Opening Remarks and Blessing
2. Explanation of the Huppah
3. Remembering Loved Ones Who Have Died
4. Blessing over the Wine: All the parents drink from one cup. The couple themselves drink from another cup.
5. Rabbi's Remarks
6. Circling

7. Exchange of Vows
8. Exchange of Rings
9. Seven Wedding Blessings Written by the Couple
10. Pronouncement
11. Benediction
12. Explanation of the Yichud
13. Breaking of the Glass

OPENING REMARKS AND BLESSINGS

Rabbi:

Welcome family and friends. (Bride) and (groom) are happy that all of you are here to share and celebrate their wedding this day. You have been such an integral part of their lives that they cannot tell you how much it means to them that you are here. They are thankful for the love and support you have given. Your role here today is not a passive one; you are encouraged not only to rejoice and honor the bride and groom on their wedding day, but also to remain a sustaining community for them.

Blessings upon all of you.

בְּרוּכִים הַבָּאִים בְּשֵׁם יְיָ.

Blessed be you who have come here in dedication to all that is loving, good, and sacred.

עִבְדוּ אֶת יְיָ בְּשִׂמְחָה. בֹּאוּ לְפָנָיו בִּרְנָנָה.

We bless you and welcome you in joy.

מִי אַדִּיר עַל הַכֹּל. מִי בָּרוּךְ עַל הַכֹּל. מִי גָדוֹל עַל הַכֹּל.
הוּא יְבָרֵךְ אֶת-הֶחָתָן וְאֶת-הַכַּלָּה.

May the Source of life sustain you in life. May all that is noble and true in the universe inspire your lives together and bring peace to all humankind.[4]

EXPLANATION OF THE HUPPAH

Rabbi:
The huppah is the Jewish symbol of the home that (bride) and (groom) are creating together. Its four sides are open, symbolizing the importance of community in their lives. Friends and family fill the home. All huppahs are special, but this one has even more meaning to (bride) and (groom) because the structure was made by (name of the person who made the huppah).

[Explanation of significance of the special ritual objects in the ceremony.]

ACKNOWLEDGING LOVED ONES WHO HAVE DIED

Rabbi:
I would also like to take this moment to remember those who are no longer with us but whose lives and spirits have touched our hearts. Let us remember them now in a moment of silence.

BLESSING OVER THE WINE

Rabbi:
Two thoughts are suggested by this cup of wine. The first is the symbol of the sweetness we wish for your life. There will be times when you drink from other cups, bitter ones, but life more often offers the opportunity to savor sweetness. The awareness of the possibility of a life filled with true meaning is what we toast: the good that is life.

The second thought is that this cup of wine honors the loving care and teaching of parents, the ties of heart and mind and memory that link family members, and the friendships that fill this cup to overflowing.
(Rabbi Wolli Kaetler)

בָּרוּךְ אַתָּה יְיָ אֱלוֹהֵינוּ מֶלֶךְ הָעוֹלָם בּוֹרֵא פְּרִי הַגָּפֶן.

Blessed are you, Adonai [this is another word for God] our God, Ruler of the universe, Creator of the fruit of the vine.

[*Hand the glass to the bride first. She gives the cup to his parents, then the groom hands the cup to her parents. Then the bride and groom take a sip from their own cup.*]

REMARKS
The rabbi's personal remarks to the bride and groom.

CIRCLING

Rabbi:
It is a very old Jewish folk custom for the bride to circle the groom during the wedding ceremony. The circle was believed to create an invisible wall of protection for them from evil spirits. The circle also symbolized the new relationship of the bride and groom, each now becoming the center of the other's attention. Today, after reciting a beautiful marriage vow from the Book of Hosea, (bride) and (groom) will circle each other one time as a sign of respect for each other's individuality, as a symbol of their appreciation of their differences, which enrich their lives, and as a sign of their love. As the Cabalists, or Jewish mystics, claim, this circling helps each of them enter the spheres of the other's soul.

EXCHANGE OF VOWS

Rabbi:
Now I ask you to face one another as you exchange your vows.

> *Groom/bride:*
> And I will betroth you to me forever. I will betroth you to me
> in righteousness, and in justice, and in loving kindness, and
> in compassion; and I will betroth you to me in faithfulness.
>
> (Hosea 2:19)

CIRCLING

The bride and groom circle one time around each other.

EXCHANGE OF RINGS

Rabbi:

These rings in their unbroken wholeness are tokens of your union and of your love. They represent the enduring trust and affection that you bring to one another. May they ever remind you that your lives are bound together by devotion, faithfulness, and an inner spiritual bond.

It is a custom to place the ring on the index finger. According to legend, the index finger contains an artery that connects directly to the heart. So as the bride and groom exchange rings, they symbolically join their hearts to one another.

(Groom), as you place the ring on (bride)'s finger, repeat after me: By this ring, you are consecrated to me as my wife according to our beliefs and in honor of ancient customs.

(Bride), as you place the ring on (groom)'s finger, repeat after me:

הֲרֵי אַתָּה מְקֻדָּשׁ לִי בְּטַבַּעַת זוֹ לְפִי אֱמוּנָתֵינוּ וּלְפִי הַמִּנְהָג.

By this ring, you are consecrated to me as my husband according to our beliefs and in honor of ancient customs.

[In this service, only the Jewish partner recites the Hebrew.]

SEVEN WEDDING BLESSINGS

Rabbi:

Historically, brides and grooms have been blessed with seven wedding blessings. The number seven is very powerful in Jewish mysticism. According to the Bible, God created the world in seven days; and marriage is a seven-day-a-week creation. As a man and woman join together in love, they make each other feel more complete and whole. For their ceremony, (bride) and (groom) have chosen to write six of their own blessings, blessings that reflect important values that give their lives meaning. The seventh blessing, the blessing over the wine, symbolically sanctifies this day and this marriage.

[Each blessing is read by a different person.]

Blessing for the Earth, Environment, and Nature
Nature and the environment provide sustenance for our bodies and spirit. Land, air, water, all living creatures and plants bring us great joy. Our appreciation of nature reveals an essence of ourselves.

Blessing for the Diversity of Humankind
The recognition of differences in each other as well as the recognition of the things we have in common helps us to appreciate the diversity and commonality we find in all humankind. We are challenged to respect each other for those differences. We learn tolerance through our relationship and the understanding of difference makes our lives richer.

Blessing for Peace and Freedom for All People
We are fortunate to live our lives in peace and freedom and we wish for a world free from suffering and oppression. May the actions we take in our lives contribute to the making of a better world.

Blessed Is the Joy of Art and Music
We are blessed with art and music. They add joy and fulfillment to our lives. Through the making of art we become in touch with ourselves, through the sharing of art we are brought closer to each other and to our fellow human beings.

Blessing for Family and Friends
We are grateful for the love and support of our parents, families, and friends: love that is expressed in laughter and through tears, and support that is founded on trust and respect. We wish good health, long life, and much happiness for all those we love.

Blessing for the Couple
Bless (bride) and (groom) in their life and home together.[5]

Blessing of the Wine

> *Rabbi:*

בָּרוּךְ אַתָּה יְיָ אֱלֹהֵינוּ מֶלֶךְ הָעוֹלָם בּוֹרֵא פְּרִי הַגָּפֶן.

Blessed are you, Adonai our God, Ruler of the universe, Creator of the fruit of the vine.

> *[Drink from the second cup of wine.]*

PRONOUNCEMENT

Rabbi:

Your friends and family, all of us here, rejoice in your happiness and we pray that this day marks only one of many more blessings you will share in the days and years ahead. And now that you have spoken the words and performed the rites that unite your lives, we now, by the power of your love and the commitment you have made, declare you, (groom) and (bride), husband and wife.

> *[Bride and groom kiss.]*

BENEDICTION

> *Rabbi:*

יְבָרֶכְךָ יְיָ וְיִשְׁמְרֶךָ.

May God bless you and keep you.

יָאֵר יְיָ פָּנָיו אֵלֶיךָ וִיחֻנֶּךָּ.

May God's presence shine upon you and be gracious to you.

יִשָּׂא יְיָ פָּנָיו אֵלֶיךָ וְיָשֵׂם לְךָ שָׁלוֹם.

May God's presence be with you and give you peace.

THE YICHUD

Rabbi:
I would like to take this opportunity to mention to you, the guests, that (bride) and (groom) will be spending a few moments alone together immediately following the ceremony. This is a custom called Yichud, which means union, in Hebrew. It gives the couple an opportunity to share, privately, the power and importance of this moment in their lives. They will return shortly to greet you.

BREAKING OF THE GLASS

Rabbi:
We end the ceremony with the traditional breaking of the glass. (Bride and/or groom) will break this second cup of wine that we used to sanctify this marriage.

*[Pour any extra wine from the cup into a bowl,
then wrap the glass in a cloth napkin.]*

Breaking this glass symbolizes the permanent change this marriage covenant makes in (bride) and (groom)'s lives.[6]

[Bride and groom kiss.]

Two Ceremonies Between a Catholic and a Jew

The Wedding Ceremony of Phil Samson
and Martha Sperry

Co-officiated by a Rabbi and a Priest
(Time: approximately 45 minutes)

1. Opening Remarks
2. Explanation of Huppah Led by the Rabbi
3. Remembering Loved Ones Who Have Died Led by the Rabbi
4. Opening Blessing by the Priest
5. Acknowledging the Two Different Traditions Led by the Priest
6. Marriage Prayer Led by the Priest
7. Sign of Peace Led by the Priest
8. Marriage Prayer and Blessing (Shehecheyanu) Led by the Rabbi
9. Marriage Prayer for the Couple Led by the Priest
10. Rabbi's Remarks
11. The Jewish Seven Wedding Blessings Led by the Rabbi
12. Blessing over the Wine Led by the Rabbi
13. Readings (read by different people)
14. Priest's Remarks
15. Declaration of Consent and Exchange of Vows Led by the Priest
16. Exchange of Rings Led by the Rabbi
17. Lighting of the Unity Candle Led by the Priest
18. Pronouncement Led by the Rabbi

19. Closing Prayers by the Rabbi and Priest
20. Breaking of the Glass Led by the Rabbi

OPENING REMARKS

Rabbi:
We are here to celebrate the love and commitment of (bride) and (groom) to one another, an occasion of great joy for all who are gathered here. They have pledged to continue the convenant, which does not begin today, but which began in wonder some time ago when they found love in each other.

EXPLANATION OF THE HUPPAH

Rabbi:
(Bride) and (groom) are standing under a huppah, which represents the promise of the home they will create together. Its four sides are open, symbolizing the importance of community and participation in each other's lives. The members of their families stand at the wall and corners of their symbolic home; they are the foundation upon which the structure of their lives rests.

ACKNOWLEDGING LOVED ONES WHO HAVE DIED

Rabbi:
The roof is made of a tallis, which represents the importance of what is beyond ourselves and the presence in our hearts of those whom we love who cannot rejoice with us today.

MARRIAGE PRAYER

Priest:
Father, hear our prayers for (bride) and (groom), who today are united in marriage. Give them your blessing and strengthen their love for each other. We ask you this through our God. (Bride) and (groom) have created this ceremony by weaving together the threads of their two traditions, a fabric that represents who they are together. In their lives and in

this ceremony they have sought to concentrate on those aspects of each other's beliefs that are shared in common and to learn as much as possible about the other's traditions.

SIGN OF PEACE

Priest:
Let us offer each other a sign of Peace. The Peace of the Lord be with you always.

Response:
And also with you.

> *[Guests turn to those seated near them to introduce themselves and to offer words of peace.]*

MARRIAGE PRAYER AND BLESSING

Rabbi:

בָּרוּךְ אַתָּה יְיָ מְקַדֵּשׁ עַמּוֹ עַל-יְדֵי חֻפָּה וְקִדּוּשִׁין.

We praise you, O God, who sanctifies your children by the holy covenant of marriage.

בָּרוּךְ אַתָּה יְיָ אֱלֹהֵינוּ מֶלֶךְ הָעוֹלָם שֶׁהֶחֱיָנוּ וְקִיְּמָנוּ וְהִגִּיעָנוּ לִזְמַן הַזֶּה.

Blessed are you, O God, for giving life, sustaining us, and bringing us to this joyous time.

MARRIAGE PRAYER

Priest:
Awed by the many meanings of this hour and overjoyed by its promises, we hope the spirit of trust, understanding, and love may be with (bride)

and (groom) through all the years that lie ahead. Whatever trials and testings may come, may they trust each other wholly, for without such faith, marriage is a mockery. May they understand each other, for without understanding there is neither acceptance nor forgiveness; and may they truly love each other, for without love, marriage is only an empty shell.

As they build together a new life and new home, may that home be bright with the laughter of children and of many friends; may it be a haven from the tensions of our time and a wellspring of strength; and in all the world, may it be the one place they most want to be, the place where they discover the ultimate human mystery, the secret of how to become one.

RABBI'S REMARKS
The rabbi's personal remarks to the bride and groom.

SEVEN WEDDING BLESSINGS

Rabbi:
In the Jewish tradition, brides and grooms are blessed with seven wedding blessings. Six of these blessings thank God for creating the world, man and woman, peace and harmony, and the joy of the bride and groom. The seventh, the blessing over the wine, sanctifies this day and this marriage.

(Bride) and (groom) I bless you now with one interpretation of these blessings.

> Cherished be the earth, the provider of all things.
> Cherished be the hopes and aspirations of friends and family.
> May we respect the diversity of humankind.
> May we acknowledge the cyclical nature of life.
> May we acknowledge the human need for providing a home.
> Honored be the tradition of bride and groom and their
>   happiness at this rite of passage that is celebrated the
>   world over.
> Praised be the sounds of joy and happiness, the voice of the

groom and the voice of the bride, the shouts of young people celebrating, and songs of children at play. We praise the bride and groom rejoicing together.

BLESSING OVER THE WINE

Rabbi:
The blessing over the wine, known as the kiddush, is a part of many Jewish celebrations and holidays. The word *kiddush* means sanctification, so the wedding is symbolically sanctified with this blessing.

The cup of wine is symbolic of the cup of life. As you share this cup of wine, you undertake to share all the future may bring. May you find life's joys doubly gladdened, its bitterness sweetened, and all things hallowed by true companionship and love.

Two cups are before you. One of these cups belongs to you (bride or groom); it was given to you by (name). The second cup belongs to both of you, jointly, and has been given to you by (name of the person who gave the bride and groom the cup). This second cup is inscribed with both of your names and indicates today's date. By your choice, only one of these cups is reserved for the two of you alone. You decided to share the first cup with those who have been partners in your lives thus far, the ones who have helped make you the individuals you are, your parents.

[Invite parents forward to share a cup of wine.]

This cup of wine symbolizes the gratitude (bride) and (groom) have for the loving care and teaching of parents, the ties of heart and mind and memory that link brothers and sisters, and the friendships that fill this cup to overflowing.

בָּרוּךְ אַתָּה יְיָ אֱלֹהֵינוּ מֶלֶךְ הָעוֹלָם בּוֹרֵא פְּרִי הַגָּפֶן.

Blessed are you, Adonai, our God, Ruler of the universe, Creator of the fruit of the vine.

READINGS

Reader:
I do not love you as if you were salt-rose, or topaz,
or the arrow of carnations the fire shoots off.
I love you as certain dark things are to be loved,
in secret, between the shadow and the soul.

I love you as the plant that never blooms
but carries in itself the light of hidden flowers;
thanks to your love a certain solid fragrance,
risen from the earth, lives darkly in my body.

I love you without knowing how, or when, or from where.
I love you straightforwardly, without complexities or pride;
so I love you because I know no other way

than this: where *I* does not exist, nor *you,*
so close that your hand on my chest is my hand,
so close that your eyes close as I fall asleep.

("Sonnet XVII," from *100 Love Sonnets:*
Cien Sonetos de amor, by Pablo Neruda)[1]

Reader:
O my dove, in the clefts of the rock,
Hidden by the cliff,
Let me see your face,
Let me hear your voice;
For your voice is sweet
and your face is beautiful.

My beloved is mine
And I am his.

(Song of Songs 2:13–14, 16)

PRIEST'S REMARKS
The priest's personal remarks to the bride and groom.

EXCHANGE OF VOWS

Priest:
(Bride) and (groom), have you come here fully and without reservation to give yourselves to each other in marriage?

Bride and groom:
We have.

Priest:
Will you love and honor each other as husband and wife for the rest of your lives?

Bride and groom:
We will.

Priest:
Since it is your intention to enter into this marriage, join your right hands and declare your consent before God.
   (Groom), do you take (bride) to be your wife; do you promise to be true to her in good times and in bad, in sickness and in health, to love her and honor her all the days of your life?

Groom:
I do.

Priest:
And do you, (bride), take (groom) to be your husband; do you promise to be true to him in good times and in bad, in sickness and in health, to love him and honor him all the days of your life?

Bride:
I do.

Priest:
You have now declared your consent before God. May God, in His goodness, strengthen your consent and fill you both with His blessing. What God has joined, let no one divide.

EXCHANGE OF RINGS

Rabbi:
We have all witnessed your exchange of vows. Yet, words are fleeting, and the sound of them will soon be gone. Therefore, the wedding rings become enduring symbols of the promises you have made to each other. The wedding rings are regarded as fitting symbols of marriage, for they are fashioned to have neither beginning nor end. The wedding rings are outward and visible symbols of your inner, spiritual bond.

(Groom), repeat after me: (Bride), I join my life with yours and offer myself into your loving care.

הֲרֵי אַתְּ מְקֻדֶּשֶׁת לִי בְּטַבַּעַת זוֹ לְפִי הַמִּנְהַג.

Be consecrated to me, as my wife, according to ancient customs.

With this ring, I join my life with yours.

אֲנִי לְדוֹדִי וְדוֹדִי לִי.

I am my beloved's and my beloved is mine.

(Bride), repeat after me: (Groom), I join my life with yours and offer myself into your loving care.

הֲרֵי אַתָּה מְקֻדָּשׁ לִי בְּטַבַּעַת זוֹ לְפִי הַמִּנְהַג.

Be consecrated to me, as my husband, according to ancient customs.

With this ring, I join my life with yours.

אֲנִי לְדוֹדִי וְדוֹדִי לִי.

I am my beloved's and my beloved is mine.

LIGHTING THE UNITY CANDLE

Priest:

In the wedding liturgy, candlelight symbolizes the commitment of love these two people have declared today.

Before you, you see three special candles. The two smaller candles symbolize the lives of the bride and groom. Until today, both have let their light shine as individuals in their respective communities. Now they publicly proclaim their love in the new union of marriage. They light the large center candle from the smaller candles to symbolize this new reality.

The connection between the flame and the human spirit as symbolized by the candle lighting is well stated in the following:

> A man from a town of Negua, on the coast of Colombia, could climb into the sky. On his return, he described his trip. He told how he had contemplated human life from on high. He said we are a sea of tiny flames. Each person shines with his or her own light. No two flames are alike. There are big flames and little flames, flames of every color. Some people's flames are so still they don't even flicker in the wind while others have wild flames that fill the air with sparks. Some foolish flames neither burn nor shed light, but blaze with life so fiercely that you can't look at them without blinking and if you approach, you shine in fire.
>
> ("The World," by Eduardo Galeano,
> translated by Cedric Belfrage)

PRONOUNCEMENT

Rabbi:

Your friends and family, all of us here, rejoice in your happiness and we pray that this day marks only one of many more blessings you will share in the days and years ahead. And now that you have spoken the words and performed the rites that unite your lives, we do hereby, in conformity with your beliefs and the laws of this state, declare your marriage to be valid and binding, and I now declare you, (groom) and (bride), husband and wife.

[Bride and groom kiss.]

CLOSING PRAYERS

Priest:
The wedding is not over, it is just begun. Not once and forever, but again and again shall the mystery of two people, together and in love, move each other and touch the world. For marriage is not something said and done, but a promise, whose fulfillment is acted out in time. Truth remains elusive, death a secret, love a challenge; life goes on neither more nor less incidentally than before, but one's hand is strengthened, one's way brightened, and one's load, if not lightened, is made easier to bear.

[Music.]

Rabbi and priest alternate:

יִהְיֶה דַרְכְּךָ מְבוֹרָךְ.

May your way be blessed.

יָאֵר אֵלֶיךָ אוֹר הַחָכְמָה.

May wisdom's light shine upon you.

יָבִיאוּ לְךָ מַסָּעֲךָ שָׁלוֹם.

May your journey bring you peace.

BREAKING OF THE GLASS

Rabbi:

It is a Jewish custom to end the wedding ceremony with the breaking of a glass. We do not know the exact origin of the custom. Some people say that the breaking of the glass symbolizes the irrevocable change in the lives of the couple standing under the huppah; others say it has its roots in superstition when people broke glasses to scare away evil spirits from such lucky people as the bride and groom. Whatever its beginnings, the breaking of the glass now has many interpretations, one of which says that even in the moment of our greatest joy, we should remember that there is still pain and suffering in the world, and that we have a responsibility to help relieve some of that pain and suffering. And, of course, the breaking of the glass marks the beginning of the celebration.[2]

[Bride and groom kiss.]

The Wedding Ceremony of Anita Seifert and Steve Georgon

Co-officiated by a Priest and Rabbi
(Time: approximately 35 minutes)

1. Opening Remarks and Blessing by the Rabbi
2. Remembering Loved Ones Who Have Died Led by the Rabbi
3. Acknowledging the Two Traditions of the Couple Led by the Rabbi
4. Opening Blessing by the Priest
5. Marriage Blessing by the Rabbi
6. Rabbi's Remarks
7. Blessing over the Wine Led by the Rabbi
8. Readings
9. Remarks by the Priest
10. Exchange of Vows Led by the Priest
11. Exchange of Rings Led by the Rabbi
12. Lighting of the Unity Candle Led by the Priest

13. Pronouncement Led by the Priest
14. Benediction Led by the Priest and Rabbi
15. Breaking of the Glass Led by the Rabbi

OPENING REMARKS AND BLESSING

Rabbi:
Welcome family and friends. (Bride) and (groom) are happy that so many of you who mean so much to them are here to share and celebrate this, their wedding day. I welcome you and bless you with these words:

> Blessed be you who have come here in dedication to all that is loving, good, and sacred.
>
> We bless you and welcome you in joy.
>
> May the Source of life sustain you in life.
>
> May all that is noble and true in the universe inspire your lives together and bring peace to all humankind.
>
> (Excerpt from Samuel Glasner,
> *The Equivocal Wedding Service*)

REMEMBERING LOVED ONES WHO HAVE DIED

Rabbi:
There are also those close to (bride) and (groom) who are not here today, but who would be rejoicing with them if they were. Let us think of them now in a moment of silence.

ACKNOWLEDGING THE BRIDE'S AND GROOM'S TRADITIONS

Rabbi:
Out of two different and distinct traditions, they have come together to learn the best of what each has to offer, appreciating their differences and

confirming that being together is far better than being apart from each other. As we bless this marriage under a huppah, the Jewish symbol of the new home being consummated here, we will later light the unity candle, a Christian symbol of two people becoming one in marriage.

PRIEST'S OPENING BLESSING

The priest gave an extemporaneous blessing.

RABBI'S MARRIAGE BLESSING

בְּרוּכִים הַבָּאִים בְּשֵׁם יְיָ.

Blessed are you who come here in the name of God.

עִבְדוּ אֶת יְיָ בְּשִׂמְחָה. בֹּאוּ לְפָנָיו בִּרְנָנָה.

Serve God with joy, come into God's presence with song.

מִי אַדִּיר עַל הַכֹּל. מִי בָּרוּךְ עַל הַכֹּל. מִי גָדוֹל עַל הַכֹּל. הוּא יְבָרֵךְ אֶת-הֶחָתָן וְאֶת-הַכַּלָּה.

O most awesome, glorious and blessed God, grant your blessings to the bride and groom.

RABBI'S REMARKS

The rabbi's personal remarks to the bride and groom.

BLESSING OVER THE WINE

Rabbi:

Two thoughts are suggested by this cup of wine. The first is that wine is a symbol of the sweetness we wish for your life. There will be times when you drink from other cups, from bitter ones; but life offers opportunity to savor the sweetness. The awareness of the possibility of a life filled with true meaning is what we toast: the good that is life. The second is that wine is a symbol of sharing. You have shared many years together, and out of this time has grown the love that brought you to this day. As you continue to share in each other's life, you will, as a symbol of this enduring cooperation, share this cup of wine.

בָּרוּךְ אַתָּה יְיָ אֱלֹהֵינוּ מֶלֶךְ הָעוֹלָם בּוֹרֵא פְּרִי הַגָּפֶן.

Blessed are you, O God, Creator of the fruit of the vine.

READING

Friend or family member:
There's no other love in the world like yours.
There's no other life like the one you will share . . .
As two pebbles in a pool spread ripples forever outward,
Your two lives will blend into one and widen and grow
    through all the days of your love,
But each of you will still be you,

Two people, separate, original and independent, even in your
    togetherness.
Just as the flame of two candles can burn apart from one
    another and yet blend their light to brighten the same room,
You will be as one and still be two.

A wonderful adventure awaits you as you go forward from
    today to build a world as wide as your wishes and as dear as
    your dreams.
It will be a world where even problems can bring you closer
    as you solve them together.
A world where you can live the story of your love, a story
    that's never before been told.
You've already shared so much from the time when you
    first met . . .
And your marriage is the beginning of a deeper sharing, a
    wider awareness, a greater happiness,
As you gaze outward in the same direction and look inward
    at the feelings that are closest to your heart.
There's no other love in the world like yours.

There's no other life like the one you will share.
And there's no joy to compare with the kind you've wished
for today, tomorrow, and always.

(Author unknown)

READING

Friend or family member:
If I have all the eloquence of men, women, or of angels, but speak without love, I am simply a gong booming or a cymbal clashing.

If I have the gift of prophecy, understanding all mysteries and knowing everything, and if I have all faith so as to move mountains, but am without love, I gain nothing.

If I give away all I possess, and if I deliver my body to be burned, but am without love, I gain nothing.

Love is always patient and kind; it is never jealous or selfish, it does not take offense and is not resentful.

Love takes not pleasure in other people's sins, but delights in the truth. It is always ready to excuse, to trust, and to endure whatever comes. Love does not end.

There are in the end three things that last: Faith, Hope, and Love, and the greatest of these is Love.

(1 Corinthians 12:31–13:8a)

PRIEST'S REMARKS
The priest spoke to the couple and the guests about the nature of love and marriage.

EXCHANGE OF VOWS

Priest:
And now your vows to each other. (Groom) and (bride), repeat after me:

Groom/Bride:
As I have come of my own free will, I promise to love and respect you, laugh with you, share my life openly and honestly

with you, support you in times of sadness, and share your joy in times of triumph. I also promise to honor and cherish you all the days of our lives.

EXCHANGE OF RINGS

Rabbi:
These rings in their unbroken wholeness are tokens of the continuity of your love. May their shining substance be a symbol of the enduring trust and affection that you bring to one another.
    (Groom), place the ring on (bride)'s finger and repeat after me:

> With this ring, I pledge my constant and abiding love.
> I join my life with yours in loving kindness and compassion.
> I join my life with yours in faithfulness.
> This is my beloved, and this is my friend.

    (Bride), place the ring on (groom)'s finger and repeat after me:

> With this ring, I pledge my constant and abiding love.
> I join my life with yours in loving kindness and compassion.
> I join my life with yours in faithfulness.
> This is my beloved, and this is my friend.

LIGHTING THE UNITY CANDLE

Priest:
From every human being there rises a light that reaches straight to heaven. And when two souls are destined to find each other, their two streams of light flow together and a single brighter light goes forth from their united being. (Baal Shem Tov)
    They do not lose their individuality; yet, in marriage, they are united in so close a bond that they become one. Now, following the profession of their marriage vows, they will light the large center candle from the smaller candles to symbolize this new reality. In this way, they are saying that henceforth their light must shine together for each other, for their families, and for their community.

PRONOUNCEMENT

Priest:
Your friends and family, all of us here, rejoice in your happiness and we pray that this day marks only one of many more blessings you will share in the days and years ahead. And now that you have spoken the words and performed the rites that unite your lives, we now, by the power of your love and the commitment you have made, declare your marriage to be valid and binding, and declare you, (groom) and (bride), husband and wife.

BENEDICTION

Rabbi and priest alternate:

יְבָרֶכְךָ יְיָ וְיִשְׁמְרֶךָ.

May God bless you and keep you.

יָאֵר יְיָ פָּנָיו אֵלֶיךָ וִיחֻנֶּךָ.

May God's countenance shine upon you and be gracious to you.

יִשָּׂא יְיָ פָּנָיו אֵלֶיךָ וְיָשֵׂם לְךָ שָׁלוֹם.

May God look upon you with favor and grant you peace.

BREAKING OF THE GLASS

Rabbi:
We conclude this ceremony with the breaking of the glass. It is a joyous ceremony. The fragility of the glass suggests the frailty of human relationships. The glass is broken to protect this marriage with the implied prayer:

May your bond of love be as difficult to break as it would be to put together the pieces of this glass.

After (groom and/or bride) breaks the glass, I invite everyone to shout the Hebrew words "Mazel Tov," which means "Good Luck" and "Congratulations."[3]

Two Ceremonies Between a Protestant and a Jew

The Wedding Ceremony of Kimberly Zolkoski and Richard Lazarus

Co-officiated by a Priest and a Rabbi
(Time: approximately 35 minutes)

1. Opening Remarks and Blessings by the Rabbi and Priest
2. Questions by the Priest
3. Explanation of Huppah by the Rabbi
4. Remembering Loved Ones Who Have Died by the Priest
5. Readings
6. Music: "Amazing Grace"
7. Exchange of Vows Led by the Priest
8. Exchange of Rings Led by the Rabbi
9. Seven Wedding Blessings, including the Blessing over the Wine, by the Rabbi
10. Concluding Prayer by the Priest
11. Pronouncement by the Priest
12. Benediction Led by the Rabbi and the Priest
13. Breaking of the Glass Led by the Rabbi

OPENING REMARKS

Priest:

Dearly beloved, we have come together in the presence of God to witness and bless the joining of this man and this woman in holy matrimony. The bond and covenant of marriage was established by God in creation and both Christian and Hebrew Holy Scriptures commend it to be honored among all people.

The union of husband and wife in heart, body, and mind is intended by God for their mutual joy; for the help and comfort given each other in prosperity and adversity; and when it is God's will for the procreation of children and their nurture in the knowledge and love of God. Therefore, marriage is not to be entered into unadvisedly or lightly, but reverently, deliberately, and in accordance with the purposes for which it was instituted by God.

Rabbi:

Adonai,[1] our God, at this sacred moment we pray for your blessings upon these, your children. They come into your presence with precious gifts; their love, their hopes and dreams, their faith in each other, and their trust in you. As they consecrate these gifts to your service, we pray that they may find life's deepest meaning and richest happiness. Bind their lives together, O God, in sanctity and in devotion. Teach them to ennoble life as they share their love.

QUESTIONS

Priest:

In this holy union (bride) and (groom) now come to be joined. If any of you can show just cause why they may not lawfully be married, speak now; or else hold your peace.

(Bride), will you have (groom) to be your husband, to live together in the covenant of marriage? Will you love him, comfort him, honor and keep him, in sickness and in health, and, forsaking all others, be faithful to him as long as you both shall live?

Bride:
I will.

Priest:
(Groom), will you have (bride) to be your wife, to live together in the covenant of marriage? Will you love her, comfort her, honor and keep her, in sickness and in health, and, forsaking all others, be faithful to her as long as you both shall live?

Groom:
I will.

Priest:
Will all of you witnessing these promises do all in your power to uphold (bride) and (groom) in their marriage?

Guests:
We will.

EXPLANATION OF THE HUPPAH

Rabbi:
We praise you, Adonai our God, Ruler of the universe, who has made us holy through your commandments. You teach us to rejoice with the bride and groom, to celebrate their consecration to each other, to witness their vows to each other, here beneath the huppah, a wedding canopy that symbolizes the new home they are creating. You are Holy, Adonai our God, and you sanctify the union of your children, (bride) and (groom), beneath the canopy.

REMEMBERING LOVED ONES WHO HAVE DIED

Priest:
There are those close to (bride) and (groom) who are not here today, but who would rejoice with them if they were. Let us think of them now in a moment of silence.

RABBI'S REMARKS

The rabbi's personal remarks to the bride and groom.

READINGS

Rabbi:
Do not press me to leave you
or to turn back from following you!
Where you go, I will go;
where you lodge, I will lodge;
Your people shall be my people,
And your God, my God.

(Ruth 1:16)

Priest:
And I will betroth you unto me forever;
I will betroth you unto me in righteousness and justice, in
steadfast love, and in mercy.
I will betroth you unto me in faithfulness. . . .

(Hosea 2:19)

PRIEST'S REMARKS

The priest spoke to the couple and the guests about love and marriage.

[Music: "Amazing Grace"]

EXCHANGE OF VOWS

Priest:
(Groom), repeat after me: In the name of God, I, (groom), take you, (bride), to be my wife, to have and to hold from this day forward, for better, for worse, for richer or poorer, in sickness and in health, to love and to cherish, until we are parted by death. This is my solemn vow.

(Bride), repeat after me: In the name of God, I, (bride), take you, (groom), to be my husband, to have and to hold from this day forward, for better, for worse, for richer or poorer, in sickness and in health, to love and to cherish, until we are parted by death. This is my solemn vow.

EXCHANGE OF RINGS

Rabbi:
In keeping with the declaration you have made, you give and receive these rings. They are tokens of your union, symbols of enduring loyalty. May they ever remind you that your lives are bound together by devotion and faithfulness.

As you, (groom), place the ring on the finger of your bride, speak to her these words:

> With this ring, be consecrated to me, as my wife, as is customary.

As you, (bride), place the ring upon your bridegroom's finger as a token of wedlock, say to him these words:

> I am my beloved's and my beloved is mine.

From every human being there rises a light that reaches straight to heaven. And when two souls are destined to find each other, their two streams of light flow together and a single brighter light goes forth from their united being. (Baal Shem Tov)

SEVEN WEDDING BLESSINGS

Rabbi:
In the Jewish tradition, brides and grooms are blessed with seven wedding blessings. Six of these blessings thank God for creating the world, man and woman, peace and harmony, and the joy of the bride and groom. The seventh, the blessing over the wine, symbolically sanctifies this day and this marriage.

As I recite these blessings, we pray that God will grant you fulfillment and joy.

> We praise you, Adonai our God, Ruler of the universe, who has created all things for your glory.

We praise you, Adonai our God, Ruler of the universe, Creator of man and woman.

We praise you, Adonai our God, Ruler of the universe, who has fashioned us in your own image and has established marriage for the fulfillment and perpetuation of life in accordance with your Holy purpose.

We praise you, Adonai our God, who blesses the joy of our gathering. May rejoicing resound among your children everywhere through your love.

We praise you, Adonai our God, Ruler of the Universe, Source of all gladness and joy. Through your grace we attain affection, companionship, and peace. Grant that the love that unites this bridegroom and this bride may gladden their souls.

We praise you, Adonai our God, Ruler of the universe. Grant that there may be peace and tranquillity in their home, contentment and confidence in their hearts. We praise you, Adonai our God, who unites bridegroom and bride in holy joy.

This cup of wine is symbolic of the cup of life. As you share this cup of wine, you undertake to share all that the future may bring. May whatever bitterness it contains be less bitter because you share it together. May all the sweetness that it holds for you be sweeter because you taste it together.

בָּרוּךְ אַתָּה יְיָ אֱלֹהֵינוּ מֶלֶךְ הָעוֹלָם בּוֹרֵא פְּרִי הַגָּפֶן.

We praise you, Adonai our God, Ruler of the universe, Creator of the fruit of the vine.

[Bride and groom take a sip of wine.]

CONCLUDING PRAYER

Priest:
Let us pray . . .

Eternal God, Creator and Preserver of all life, Giver of grace; look with favor upon the world you have made and especially upon (bride) and (groom) whom you make one in holy matrimony.

Give them wisdom and devotion in the ordering of their common life, that each may be to the other a strength in need, a counselor in perplexity, a comfort in sorrow, and a companion in joy.

Grant that their wills may be knit together in your will and their spirits in your spirit, that they may grow in love and peace with you and one another all the days of their lives.

Give them grace, when they hurt each other, to recognize and acknowledge their fault, and to seek each other's forgiveness and yours.

Make their life together a sign of God's love to this sinful and broken world, that unity may overcome estrangement, forgiveness heal guilt, and joy conquer despair.

Give them such fulfillment of their mutual affection that they may reach out in love and concern for others.

Grant that all married persons who have witnessed these vows may find their lives strengthened and their loyalties confirmed.

Most gracious God, we give you thanks for your tender love. We thank you also for consecrating the union of this man and woman in your name. By your power, pour out the abundance of your blessing upon (bride) and (groom). Defend them from every enemy. Lead them into all peace. Let their love for each other be a seal upon their hearts, a mantle about their shoulders, and a crown upon their foreheads. Bless them in their work and in their companionship; in their sleeping and in their waking; in their joys and in their sorrows all the days of their life. Amen.

PRONOUNCEMENT

Priest:
Now that (bride) and (groom) have given themselves to each other by solemn vows, with the joining of hands and the giving and receiving of a ring, we pronounce that they are husband and wife in the name of God.

Those whom God has joined together, let no one put asunder.
Amen.

[Bride and groom kiss.]

BENEDICTION

Rabbi and priest, alternating:

יְבָרֶכְךָ יְיָ וְיִשְׁמְרֶךָ.

May God bless you and keep you.

יָאֵר יְיָ פָּנָיו אֵלֶיךָ וִיחֻנֶּךָ.

May God's presence shine upon you and be gracious to you.

יִשָּׂא יְיָ פָּנָיו אֵלֶיךָ וְיָשֵׂם לְךָ שָׁלוֹם.

May God's presence be with you and give you peace.

BREAKING OF THE GLASS

Rabbi:
May the breaking of this glass remind you of the fragility of human relationships. A broken glass cannot be mended, and likewise marriage is irrevocable. As this glass shatters, so may your marriage never break.
Amen.

[Bride and groom kiss.][2]

The Wedding Ceremony of JoAnn Pappalardo and Steven Cooperstein

Officiated by a Rabbi
(Time: approximately 30 minutes)

1. Opening Remarks and Blessing of the Couple
2. Remembering Loved Ones Who Have Died
3. Acknowledging the Traditions of the Couple
4. Explanation of the Huppah
5. Remarks by the Rabbi
6. Scripture Reading: Ruth 1:16
7. Music: "The Wedding Song," by Peter, Paul, and Mary
8. Scripture Reading: 1 Corinthians 12:31–13:8a
9. Marriage Blessing
10. Seven Wedding Blessings in English Only
11. Blessing over the Wine
12. Music: excerpt from *Les Miserables* "Finale"
13. Exchange of Vows
14. Exchange of Rings
15. Blessing of the Marriage
16. Lighting of the Unity Candle
17. Music: "Perhaps Love," by John Denver
18. Pronouncement
19. Closing Reading
20. Benediction
21. Breaking of the Glass

OPENING REMARKS

Rabbi:
Welcome family and friends. We are gathered together to celebrate (bride) and (groom)'s love for each other and to honor and celebrate their decision to make a lifelong commitment to each other. They are happy that so many friends and family members are here to share and celebrate with them today.

Your role here is not a passive one. You are encouraged not only to rejoice and honor the bride and groom on their wedding day, but also to remain a sustaining community for them.

(Bride) and (groom), I bless you with these traditional Hebrew words, along with an English interpretation of them.

בְּרוּכִים הַבָּאִים בְּשֵׁם יְיָ.

Blessed be you who have come here in dedication to all that is loving, good, and sacred.

עִבְדוּ אֶת יְיָ בְּשִׂמְחָה. בֹּאוּ לְפָנָיו בִּרְנָנָה.

We bless you and welcome you in joy.

מִי אַדִּיר עַל הַכֹּל. מִי בָּרוּךְ עַל הַכֹּל. מִי גָדוֹל עַל הַכֹּל. הוּא
יְבָרֵךְ אֶת-הֶחָתָן וְאֶת-הַכַּלָּה.

May the Source of life sustain you in life.
May all that is noble and true in the universe,
Inspire your lives together and bring peace to all humankind.[3]

REMEMBERING LOVED ONES WHO HAVE DIED

Rabbi:
There are also those close to (bride) and (groom) who are not here today but who would be rejoicing with them if they were. Let us remember them by thinking of them now in a moment of silence.

ACKNOWLEDGING THE TWO TRADITIONS OF THE BRIDE AND GROOM AND THE COUPLE'S ROLE IN CREATING THE SERVICE

Rabbi:
(Bride) and (groom) have created this ceremony. They have woven, from threads of two traditions, a fabric that represents who they are together. They wish to share with you their reflections on marriage and their hopes for the future.

Marriage is an extraordinary event. (Bride) and (groom) present a relationship that has been challenged by time and personal change. Their love has prevailed by virtue of its strengths. Yet marriage adds a new dimension, which they approach with enthusiasm and deepening love. Today (bride) and (groom) start a new life together, different from the togetherness they have shared so far.

EXPLANATION OF THE HUPPAH

Rabbi:
They stand under a huppah, which represents this new reality. It represents the promise of the new home they will create together. Its four sides are open, symbolizing the importance of community and participation in each other's life.

Holy One, in this sacred hour, we pray for your blessings upon these, your children. They come to you with precious gifts: their youth, their love, their hopes and dreams, their faith in each other, and their trust in you. May they consecrate these gifts unto your service and so find life's deepest meaning and richest happiness. Bind their lives together, O God, in sanctity and in devotion, and teach them to ennoble life's experiences by sharing them in love.

REMARKS (INCLUDING THE FOLLOWING . . .)

Rabbi:
Experience has taught you that not all your moments will be filled with joy. Events beyond our control will test your strength. Different values, desires, and pressures will try your patience and compassion. Yet, if you remain open and honest, even the most difficult trial will not break the bond between you. With love and trust as foundations, the storms can bring you closer together.

READING (WOVEN INTO THE REMARKS)

Rabbi:

. . . wherever you go, I will go; wherever you lodge, I will lodge; your people shall be my people, and your God my God.

(Ruth 1:16)

[Music: "The Wedding Song," by Peter, Paul, and Mary]

READING

Rabbi:

If I have all the eloquence of men, women, or of angels, but speak without love, I am simply a gong booming or a cymbal clashing.

If I have the gift of prophecy, understanding all mysteries and knowing everything, and if I have all faith so as to move mountains, but am without love, I gain nothing.

If I give away all I possess, and if I deliver my body to be burned, but am without love, I gain nothing.

Love is always patient and kind; it is never jealous or selfish, it does not take offense and is not resentful.

Love takes not pleasure in other people's sins, but delights in the truth. It is always ready to excuse, to trust, and to endure whatever comes. Love does not end.

There are in the end three things that last: Faith, Hope and Love, and the greatest of these is Love.

(1 Corinthians 12:31–13:8a)

MARRIAGE BLESSING

Rabbi:

These are our hopes for the two of you:

We hope you will use your love creatively, working toward personal and social change in the world. May you both openly give and take from each other, sharing in each other's joys and encouraging each other throughout all that your lives bring. We hope that you will continue to find in each other the resources that will nurture your marriage. We wish you a home filled with health, warmth, and children. Having grown to trust yourselves and each other, may you be unafraid to trust and welcome life.

WEDDING BLESSINGS

Rabbi:
In the Jewish tradition, brides and grooms are blessed with seven wedding blessings. They praise and celebrate God, creation, man and woman, peace and harmony, and the joy of the bride and groom. (Bride) and (Groom), I will now bless you with one version of these blessings.

> We bless God for creating the universe.
> We bless God for creating the individual.
> We bless God for creating human beings who are one at their core and who complement each other by their differences as woman and man.
> We ask that our land be happy and bless God for letting Zion rejoice with her children.
> Let these loving friends rejoice. May their joy be paradise on earth. We bless God for enabling this bride and this groom to rejoice.
> We bless God for creating joy and happiness, bride and groom, mirth song, gladness and rejoicing, love and harmony, peace and companionship; and we thank God for letting this bride and groom to rejoice together.

BLESSING OVER THE WINE

Rabbi:
This cup of wine is symbolic of the cup of life. As you share the one cup of wine, you undertake to share all that the future may bring. All the sweetness life's cup may hold for you should be sweeter because you drink it together; whatever drops of bitterness it may contain should be less bitter because you share them.

As I recite the blessing over the wine, we pray that God will bestow fullness of joy upon you.

בָּרוּךְ אַתָּה יְיָ אֱלֹהֵינוּ מֶלֶךְ הָעוֹלָם בּוֹרֵא פְּרִי הַגָּפֶן.

Blessed are you, O Lord our God, Creator of the fruit of the vine.

As together you now drink from this cup, so may you, under God's guidance, in perfect union and devotion to each other, draw contentment, comfort, and happiness from the cup of life. Thereby may you find life's joys doubly gladdening, its bitterness sweetened, and all things hallowed by true companionship and love.

[Music from Les Miserables: *"Finale"]*[4]

EXCHANGE OF VOWS

Rabbi:
(Bride) and (groom), you have pledged to share the responsibility for making this union one of equality, understanding, and strength, and you are now making your promise sacred.

Please join your right hands and declare your intentions in the presence of God and this gathering.[5]

Groom:
I (groom), take you (bride) to be my wife. I give you my hand and my love. I promise to be true to you in good times and in bad, in sickness and in health. I will love and honor you all the days of my life.

Bride:
I (bride), take you (groom) to be my husband. I give you my hand and my love. I promise to be true to you in good times and in bad, in sickness and in health. I will love and honor you all the days of my life.

EXCHANGE OF RINGS

Rabbi:
God, bless these rings that we bless in your name. Grant that those who wear them always have a deep faith in each other. May they always live together in peace, good will, and love.[6]

These rings in their unbroken wholeness are tokens of your union and of your love. They represent the enduring trust and affection that you bring to each other. May they ever remind you that your lives are bound together by devotion, faithfulness, and an inner spiritual bond.[7]

(Groom), as you place the ring on (bride)'s finger, repeat after me: With this ring I join my life with yours. I pledge my constant faith and abiding love. You are my beloved and you are my friend.

(Bride), as you place the ring on (groom)'s finger, repeat after me: With this ring I join my life with yours. I pledge my constant faith and abiding love. You are my beloved and you are my friend.

BLESSING OVER THE MARRIAGE

Rabbi:

בָּרוּךְ אַתָּה יְיָ מְקַדֵּשׁ עַמּוֹ עַל־יְדֵי חֻפָּה וְקִדּוּשִׁין.

Praised are you, O God, who sanctifies your children by the holy convenant of marriage.

LIGHTING OF THE UNITY CANDLE

Rabbi:
In the wedding liturgy, candlelight symbolizes the commitment of love these two people have declared today.

Before you, you see three special candles. The two smaller candles symbolize the lives of the bride and groom. Until today, both have let their light shine as individuals in their respective communities. Now they publicly proclaim their love in the new union of marriage. They light the large center candle from the smaller candles to symbolize this new reality.

[Light the havdalah candle. This center candle is called an havdalah candle. It is traditionally used in a Jewish ceremony to end the Sabbath on Saturday night. This special candle is made of several wicks that are braided together. It is used here for a different purpose, to symbolize the intertwining of the lives of the bride and groom. The candle also makes a very large flame, burning brighter than any individual candle. The symbolism is reflected in the quote below.]

From every human being there rises a light that reaches straight to heaven. And when two souls are destined to find one another, their two streams of light flow together and a single brighter light goes forth from their united being.

(Baal Shem Tov)

[Music: "Perhaps Love," by John Denver.
(Bride) and (groom) present roses to their mothers.]

PRONOUNCEMENT

Rabbi:
Your friends and family, all of us here, rejoice in your happiness and we pray that this day marks only one of many more blessings you will share in the days and years ahead. And now that you have spoken the words and performed the rites that unite your lives, I do hereby, in conformity with ancient customs and the laws of this state, declare your marriage to be valid and binding. By the power of your love, and the commitment you have made, I now pronounce you husband and wife.

[Bride and groom kiss.]

READING

Rabbi:
May the courage of the early morning's dawning
And the strength of the eternal hills at noontime
And the peace of the open spaces at evening's ending
And the love that abides in your hearts, now, and forever,
Bring you deep happiness. (Javanese poem)

BENEDICTION

Rabbi:

יְבָרֶכְךָ יְיָ וְיִשְׁמְרֶךָ.

May God bless you and keep you.

יָאֵר יְיָ פָּנָיו אֵלֶיךָ וִיחֻנֶּךָּ.

May God's countenance shine upon you and be gracious
to you.

יִשָּׂא יְיָ פָּנָיו אֵלֶיךָ וְיָשֵׂם לְךָ שָׁלוֹם.

May God look upon you with favor and grant you peace.

BREAKING OF THE GLASS

Rabbi:
It is a Jewish custom to end the wedding ceremony with the breaking of a
glass. We don't know the exact origins of the custom. Some believe it
has its roots in superstition, when people broke glasses to scare away evil
spirits from such fortunate people as brides and grooms. Whatever its
beginnings, the breaking of the glass now has many interpretations, one
of which says that even in the moment of our greatest joy, we should
remember that there is still pain and suffering in the world, and that we
have a responsibility to help relieve some of that pain and suffering.
Another explanation simply says that we break the glass to mark the
beginning of the celebration.

As (groom and/or bride) breaks the glass, I invite everyone to shout
"Mazel Tov," which means "Congratulations" and "Good Luck" in
Hebrew.

[Bride and groom kiss.][8]

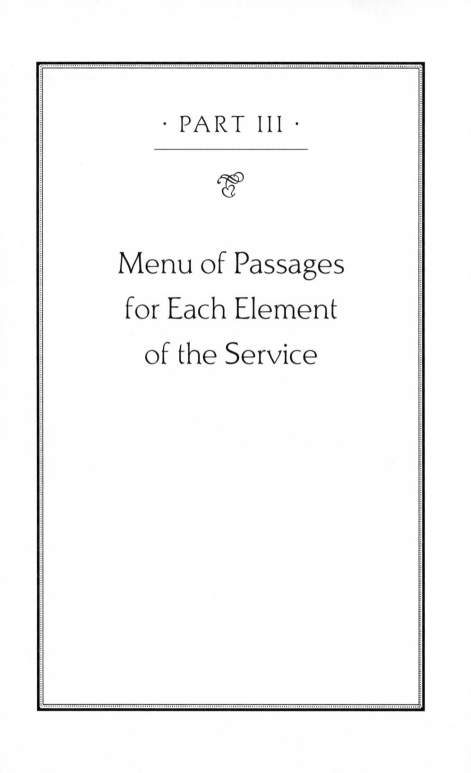

PART III

Menu of Passages
for Each Element
of the Service

This "Menu of Passages" is designed to help you create a first draft of your ceremony. The process is quite simple. In these pages, you will find a collection of passages for each of the most common elements of an interfaith ceremony. By choosing one or more passages for each element of your ceremony, and by placing them in the order they appear in this menu, you will have a first draft of your ceremony.

As you read the various selections, you will know which ones you like and dislike. You may actually find more than one passage in each section that appeals to you. At this point in the process, do not worry about the number of readings you choose or about the length of your ceremony. Simply select all the passages you like. Copy all of your choices and arrange them in the order that they appear here. This will become your first working draft of your ceremony.

With this draft in hand, you are ready to edit your selections and add any material you like that is not included in these pages. I actually encourage you to add something of your own, something that is unique to you, such as your own vows, readings, or music that has special meaning to both of you. The more you personalize your ceremony, the more meaningful it will be for you as a couple.

Opening Remarks and Blessings

☙

Your opening remarks and blessings will set the tone of your service. Many couples like to begin with an informal greeting of their guests, but some couples prefer to set a more formal religious tone by selecting opening prayers from each of their traditional wedding liturgies. Still others like to use a combination of both religious and contemporary passages. This section includes examples of each of these styles. For your ceremony, choose the approach that appeals to you, or create your own blessings and remarks by writing them yourselves or by combining and editing what you see in this section.

Selection 1
Welcome family and friends. We are gathered together to celebrate (bride/partner) and (groom/partner's) love for each other and their decision to make the lifelong commitment of marriage to each other. They have come to this ceremony under the huppah to ask God's blessing upon their marriage.

בְּרוּכִים הַבָּאִים בְּשֵׁם יְיָ.

Blessed are you who come here in the name of God.

עִבְדוּ אֶת יְיָ בְּשִׂמְחָה. בֹּאוּ לְפָנָיו בִּרְנָנָה.

Serve God with joy, come into God's presence with song.

מִי אַדִּיר עַל הַכֹּל. מִי בָּרוּךְ עַל הַכֹּל. מִי גָּדוֹל עַל הַכֹּל.
הוּא יְבָרֵךְ אֶת-הֶחָתָן וְאֶת-הַכַּלָּה.

O most awesome, glorious, and blessed God, grant your blessings to the bride and groom.

Selection 2

Welcome, family and friends. (Bride) and (groom) are happy that so many of you who mean so much to them are here to share and celebrate their wedding this day. Your role here today is not a passive one; you are encouraged not only to rejoice and honor the bride and groom on their wedding day, but also to remain a sustaining community for them.

(Bride) and (groom), I bless you with these traditional Hebrew words along with an English interpretation.

בְּרוּכִים הַבָּאִים בְּשֵׁם יְיָ.

Blessed be you who have come here in dedication to all that is loving, good, and sacred.

עִבְדוּ אֶת יְיָ בְּשִׂמְחָה. בֹּאוּ לְפָנָיו בִּרְנָנָה.

We bless you and welcome you in joy.

מִי אַדִּיר עַל הַכֹּל. מִי בָּרוּךְ עַל הַכֹּל. מִי גָּדוֹל עַל הַכֹּל. הוּא
יְבָרֵךְ אֶת-הֶחָתָן וְאֶת-הַכַּלָּה.

May the Source of life sustain you in life.
May all that is noble and true in the universe,
Inspire your lives together and bring peace to all
humankind.[1]

Selection 3

We are here at a time of happiness to celebrate (bride) and (groom)'s love and the commitment they have made to marriage. They stand under a huppah. It represents the promise of the home they will create together. Its four sides are open, symbolizing the importance of community and participation in each other's lives. Friends and family fill the home. The roof includes a tallis, which belongs to (name of person who owns the tallis). It symbolizes the importance of what is beyond ourselves and the presence, in our hearts, of those whom we love who cannot rejoice with us today.

Selection 4

We are gathered here to join (bride) and (groom) in marriage. It is fitting and appropriate that you, the family and friends, be here to witness and participate in their wedding, because the ideals, the understanding, and the mutual respect that they bring to their marriage have their roots in the love, friendship, and guidance that you have given them.

Selection 5

(Bride) and (groom) have asked us to be a part of this celebration of their love for each other, and it is with great joy and reverence that we all take part. They seek to continue the commitment, which does not begin today, but which began in wonder some time ago when they found love in each other.

There are many stages and kinds of commitment among persons in our culture, but this one is the deepest, the most sacred that comes out of the clear choice of two people. It is said that love is the communication of the good life. When we find a person who communicates the good life to us, and whose answering resonance tells us that we have been sharing something significant together, then we may make the decision to continue sharing permanently. (Bride) and (groom) have found much to share and much to enrich their lives together.[2]

Selection 6

Dearly Beloved: we have come together in the presence of God to witness and bless the joining together of this man and this woman in holy matrimony. The bond and covenant of marriage was established by God in creation, and symbolizes the covenant relationship between God and humankind. It signifies to us the mystery of the union of God and of God's people Israel, and Holy scripture commands it to be honored among all people.

The union of husband and wife in heart, body, and mind is intended by God for their mutual joy; for the help and comfort given each other in prosperity and adversity; and, when it is God's will, for the procreation of children and their nurture in the knowledge and love of God. Therefore, marriage is not to be entered into unadvisedly or lightly, but reverently, deliberately, and in accordance with the purposes for which it was instituted by God.

Into this holy union (bride) and (groom) now come to be joined. If any of you can show just cause why they may not be lawfully married, speak now; or else forever hold your peace.

I require and charge you both, here in the presence of God, that if either of you knows any reason why you may not be united in marriage lawfully, and in accordance with God's Word, you do now confess it.[3]

Explanation of the Huppah

Many interfaith couples like to be married under a huppah, the Jewish wedding canopy. If you choose to have one for your wedding, I strongly recommend that you include an explanation of the symbolism in your ceremony. You may choose a brief or more lengthy explanation. Which one is right for you may depend, in part, on your personality. If you like history, for example, you may prefer the last entry in this chapter, which gives a detailed account of much of the history and symbolism of the huppah. One groom I married felt the details added to the spiritual meaning of his ceremony. For some other interfaith couples, however, this same explanation feels too involved and too lengthy. If this is true for you, choose one of the shorter, simpler options.

Selection 1
We are here at a time of happiness to celebrate (bride) and (groom)'s love and the commitment they have made to marriage. They stand under a huppah. It represents the promise of the home they will create together. Its four sides are open, symbolizing the importance of community and participation in each other's lives. The members of their families stand at the wall and corners of their symbolic home; they are the foundation upon which the structure of their lives rests. Friends and family fill the home. The roof also includes a tallis, which belongs to (name of person who owns the tallis). It symbolizes the importance of what is beyond ourselves and the presence, in our hearts, of those whom we love who cannot rejoice with us today.

Selection 2

We bless this marriage today under a huppah, the symbol of the new home being consummated here.

Selection 3

We live in the world; most of us live in houses and apartment buildings, near busy streets. But there are two temporary structures that we build in our lifetimes. One is the succah, the desert booth. The other is the huppah, the wedding canopy.

Every year, the succah reminds us that once we had no permanent place, no land where we could sow and expect to reap at the end of a long growing season. It reminds us that once we were wanderers in the wilderness, and we longed for a home. We talk about how easily the succah collapses. It has firm walls, so that we can almost pretend that it is real, but we lay tree branches across the roof for thatch, tie paper birds and gourds from the rafters, and count the stars through the leaves.

The huppah is different. Who could mistake it for a real house? Its walls are nonexistent. The roof is flimsy. Wind can blow through the huppah. The rain is welcome. The couple who stand under its shelter must leave it to look up and see the stars.

But it is the huppah that we take for our home when we are promising each other everything. It is raised, for most of us, once in a lifetime. It is not permanent. But it is the promise of a home.

Its openness pledges that there will be no secrets. Friends and family stand at the corners, weighing the fragile structure down. The roof is often a tallit so that the bride and groom are covered by holiness and the memory of commandments.

The huppah does not promise that love or hope or pledges will keep out weather or catastrophe. But its few lines are a sketch for what might be.

The man and woman have left the desert of their loneliness. They have come from far away to be together. The flimsiness of the huppah reminds them that the only thing that is real about a home is the people in it who love and choose to be together, to be a family. The only anchor that they will have will be holding onto each others' hands.

The huppah is the house of promises. It is the home of hope.[1]

Selection 4

Long after tents vanished from the Jewish landscape, wedding ceremonies were held out of doors in the hope that the marriage would be blessed by as many children as the stars in heaven. Some kind of covering was employed to create a more modest and sanctified space.

The bridal canopy, or huppah, is a multifaceted symbol. It symbolizes modesty in the presence of God, the safety of your home, the protection of a garment, the intimacy of your bed covering.

It is open on all sides to symbolize the importance of what is beyond ourselves, and the respect of Abraham, who had doors on all four sides of his home so that visitors would always know they were welcome.[2]

The huppah does not promise that love or hope or pledges will keep out weather or catastrophe, but its few lines are a sketch for what might be. The flimsiness of the huppah is a reminder that the only thing that is real about the home is the people in it who love and choose to be together, to be a family. The only anchor that they will have will be holding on to each other's hands. The huppah is the house of promises; it is the home of hope.[3]

Acknowledging
Different Traditions

Many couples wish to include some statement about their different backgrounds and faiths in their wedding ceremony. The purpose is not to state the obvious fact that they are an interfaith couple, but to emphasize their appreciation for their own and each other's traditions.

Selection 1
(Bride) and (groom) have created this ceremony. They have woven from threads of two traditions, a fabric that represents who they are together. They wish to share with you their reflections on marriage and their hopes for the future. . . .

Selection 2
Out of two different and distinct traditions, they have come together to learn the best of what each has to offer, appreciating their differences, and confirming that being together is far better than being apart from each other. As we bless this marriage under the huppah, the Jewish symbol of the new home being consummated here, we will later light the unity candle, the Christian symbol of two people becoming one in marriage.

Selection 3
Today, (bride) and (groom) have chosen to marry. To start their new life together, they will be merging their different individual lives, their different families, and their different faiths to join each other as one.

Selection 4
God, hear our prayers for (bride) and (groom), who today are united in marriage. Give them your blessing and strengthen their love for each other. We ask You this through our God. (Bride) and (groom) have created this ceremony by weaving together the threads of their two traditions, a fabric that represents who they are together. In their lives and in this ceremony they have sought to concentrate on those aspects of each other's beliefs that are shared in common and to learn as much as possible about the other's traditions.[1]

Acknowledging Children from a Previous Marriage

If you have children from a previous marriage, I encourage you to include them in your ceremony. Younger children, especially, need some reasssurance that your new partner will not diminish your love and care for them. Keep in mind that your wedding day and ceremony can feel overwhelming to your child, so much so that it is not unusual for young children to start crying or to refuse to participate at the last minute. Be prepared to be flexible!

Older children can participate by reading a poem or passage, or they may stand next to you during the service. If none of these options appeals to you, you can simply ask your officiant to talk about your love for and connection to your children in his or her remarks.

Selection 1
This marriage joins together not just two individuals, but two families as well. The life that (bride) and (groom) and (name the children) have together will be that much richer for the unique character that each brings.

To celebrate their new family, (bride) and (groom) would like to present (name of child or children) with a symbol of their love.

[Couple presents the child or children with a gift.][1]

Selection 2

This wedding brings together not only two individuals, but two families as well. (Name of the children), you are a very important part of this celebration today and you will always be an important and central part of (name of stepparent)'s and your (father's, mother's, or parents') lives. This day is even more joyous for them because you are here.

Remembering Loved Ones
Who Have Died

There are several ways to acknowledge loved ones who have died. You may choose to mention them with one of the passages below, or you may prefer to remember them in more symbolic ways. One couple I married simply placed a small votive candle on the table holding the other ritual items. As the candle burned during their ceremony, they felt the spirits of their loved ones with them. No additional words were necessary. Some couples like to remember their loved ones by using something that belonged to them in their ceremony. One couple placed the groom's deceased grandfather's tallis on their huppah. Another couple used candlesticks that were family heirlooms.

Selection 1
There are those close to (bride) and (groom) who are not here today, but who would rejoice with them if they were. Today they especially remember (names of the deceased). Let us think of them now in a moment of silence.

Selection 2
There are also those who were close to (bride) and (groom) who have died but who we remember today, because they have been such an important part of their lives. Their spirits touched them and helped make them the individuals they are. Let us remember them now in a moment of silence.

Selection 3
The roof of the huppah symbolizes the importance of what is beyond ourselves and the presence, in our hearts, of those whom we love who cannot rejoice with us today.

or

The roof of the huppah, which includes a tallis, symbolizes the importance of what is beyond ourselves. . . .

Selection 4
I would also like to take this moment to remember those who are no longer with us but whose lives and spirits have touched our hearts. Let us remember them now in a moment of silence.

Selection 5

Zachor
Remembrance
A memory of those people who shape our lives,
whose presence wraps us in protective holiness,
an invisible tallis, all of whom are present in spirit,
always to walk around us like guardian angels.
Their names and memory a blessing
(names of loved ones listed here)
They are here and they bless this union.
Blessed be the Creative One, whose blessing
comes to us through each generation.
L'dor v'dor. Amen.[1]

General Marriage Blessings and Prayers

The following section includes several marriage blessings and prayers from both Jewish and Christian sources. You may choose one or more of these for your ceremony, and you may place them anywhere you like. At least one, however, is usually placed here, near the beginning of the service. See the sample ceremonies in Part II for more ideas for placement.

Selection 1

בָּרוּךְ אַתָּה יְיָ מְקַדֵּשׁ עַמּוֹ יִשְׂרָאֵל עַל-יְדֵי חֻפָּה וְקִדּוּשִׁין.

We praise you, Adonai our God, Ruler of the universe, who sanctifies our people Israel through kiddushin, the sacred rite of marriage at the huppah.

Selection 2

בָּרוּךְ אַתָּה יְיָ מְקַדֵּשׁ עַמּוֹ עַל-יְדֵי חֻפָּה וְקִדּוּשִׁין.

We praise you, O God, who sanctifies your children by the covenant of marriage.

Selection 3

בָּרוּךְ אַתָּה יְיָ אֱלֹהֵינוּ מֶלֶךְ הָעוֹלָם שֶׁהֶחֱיָנוּ וְקִיְּמָנוּ וְהִגִּיעָנוּ
לַזְּמַן הַזֶּה.

We praise you, O God, Ruler of the universe, who has given
us life, sustained us, and brought us to this joyous time.[1]

Selection 4

בְּרוּכִים הַבָּאִים בְּשֵׁם יְיָ.

Blessed are you who come here in the name of God.

עִבְדוּ אֶת יְיָ בְּשִׂמְחָה. בֹּאוּ לְפָנָיו בִּרְנָנָה.

Serve God with joy, come into God's presence with song.

מִי אַדִּיר עַל הַכֹּל. מִי בָּרוּךְ עַל הַכֹּל. מִי גָדוֹל עַל הַכֹּל.
הוּא יְבָרֵךְ אֶת-הֶחָתָן וְאֶת-הַכַּלָּה.

O most awesome, glorious and blessed God, grant your blessings to the bride and groom.

Selection 5

Our God, bestow your blessings upon (bride) and (groom) as they unite
their lives in your name. Cause them to prosper in their life together.
Teach them to share the joys and trials of life and to grow in understanding and in devotion. May love and companionship abide within the
home they establish. May they grow old together in health and contentment by this union of their lives.[2]

Selection 6

May they build a life together that is bright with the laughter of children
and the smiles of friends and family. May their home be a haven from the
tensions of our time and a wellspring of strength; may it be the one place
where they most want to be. And may the years deal gently with them.

Walking together, may they find much more in life than either would have found alone.

Selection 7

Despite whatever trials and challenges lie ahead, may they trust each other wholly, for without such faith, marriage is a mockery. May they understand each other, for without understanding there is neither acceptance nor forgiveness. And may they truly love each other, for without love, marriage is only an empty promise.

Selection 8

Marriage is a sacred event. (Bride) and (groom) present a relationship that has been challenged by time and personal change. Their love has prevailed by virtue of its strengths. Yet marriage adds a new dimension, which they approach with enthusiasm and deepening love. Today, (bride) and (groom) start a new life together, different from the togetherness they have shared so far.

Selection 9

Today, (bride) and (groom) have chosen to marry. To start their new life together, they will be merging their different individual lives, their different families, and their different faiths to join each other as one.

In the presence of God, our hearts are filled with great happiness on this special wedding day. (Bride) and (groom) come before us pledging their love and their hearts to one another.

May they be ever true and loving; may they fill their hearts with kindness and understanding, and forgive each other's weaknesses and laugh together often. May they be friends, companions, and partners, meeting the joys and cares of life as one. As the years pass, may their love deepen and mature, and may their home be truly a place of love and joy.

This wedding day is blessed. (Bride) and (groom), we pray that all your days together will be blessed ones.

Selection 10

O God, in this sacred hour, we pray for our blessings upon these, your children. They come to you with precious gifts: their youth, their love, their hopes and dreams, their faith in each other, and their trust in you.

May they consecrate these gifts unto your service and so find life's deepest meaning and richest happiness. Bind their lives together, O God, in sanctity and in devotion, and teach them to ennoble life's experiences by sharing them in love.

We bless this marriage today under a huppah, the symbol of the new home being consummated here.[3]

Selection 11

Awed by the many meanings of this hour and overjoyed by its promises, we hope the spirit of trust, understanding, and love may be with (bride) and (groom) through all the years that lie ahead. Whatever trials and testings may come, may they trust each other wholly, for without such faith, marriage is a mockery. May they understand each other, for without understanding there is neither acceptance nor forgiveness; and may they truly love each other, for without love, marriage is only an empty shell from which the white bird has flown.

As they build together a new life and new home, may that home be bright with the laughter of children and of many friends; may it be a haven from the tensions of our time and a wellspring of strength; and in all the world, may it be the one place they most want to be, the place where they discover the ultimate human mystery—the secret of how to become one.

So may this shining hour be an open door through which (bride) and (groom) will go forth to build that dearest of all relationships, a happy, harmonious marriage. May the years deal gently with them. Walking together, may they find far more in life than either would have found alone; and even more fully may they come to know this one supreme truth—that caring is sharing . . . that loving is giving . . . that life is eternal . . . and that love is its crown.

Selection 12

God has given us promises and (bride) and (groom) have given their promise to each other in their marriage. This hour of promise is also a time of prayer and so we turn to God and make our response by saying, "Lord, hear our prayer."

For our world, to keep the promise of peace. We pray . . .
For our hearts, to keep the promise of loving. We pray . . .
For our hands, to keep the promise of giving. We pray . . .
For our lives, to keep the promise of growing. We pray . . .
For (bride) and (groom) to keep the promise of marriage and
    commitment to each other, to their families and friends,
    and to their God. We pray . . .

Selection 13

Through love may you know the secrets of your heart and in that knowledge, your understanding of life will deepen. May you find life's richest happiness; and may your lives be bound together in sanctity and in devotion to each other, so that you ennoble all of life's experiences by sharing them in love.

Selection 14

Eternal God, creator and preserver of all life, author of salvation, and giver of all grace: Look with favor upon the world you have made, (and for which your Son gave his life), and especially upon this man and this woman whom you make one flesh in holy matrimony.

Give them wisdom and devotion in the ordering of their common life, that each may be to the other a strength in need, a counselor in perplexity, a comfort in sorrow, and a companion in joy.

Grant that their wills may be so knit together in your will, and their spirits in your Spirit, that they may grow in love and peace with you and one another all the days of their lives.

Give them grace, when they hurt each other, to recognize and acknowledge their fault, and to seek each other's forgiveness and yours.

Make their life together a song of God's love to this (sinful and) broken world, that they may overcome estrangement, forgiveness heal guilt, and joy conquer despair.

Bestow on them, if it is your will, the gift and heritage of children, and the grace to bring them up to know you, to love you and to serve you.

Give them such fulfillment of their mutual affection that they may reach out in love and concern for others.

Grant that all married persons who have witnessed these vows may find their lives strengthened and their loyalties confirmed . . .

(Excerpt from *The Book of Common Prayer*)

Selection 15
We hope you will use your love creatively, working toward personal and social change in the world. May you both openly give and take from each other, sharing in each other's joys and encouraging each other throughout all that your lives bring. We hope that you will continue to find in each other the resources that will nurture your marriage. We wish you a home filled with health, warmth, and children. Having grown to trust yourselves and each other, may you be unafraid to trust and welcome life.

Blessing over the Wine

The following selections illustrate various ways to introduce and explain the blessing over the wine. Notice that some of these explanations mention only one cup of wine, while others refer to two cups of wine. When two cups are used, one is usually shared with the bride and groom's parents, while the other cup is reserved specifically for the wedding couple. Although sharing the ritual wine with parents is not traditional, it has become a popular addition in many Jewish and interfaith wedding ceremonies.

Selection 1

This cup of wine is symbolic of the cup of life. As you share the one cup of wine, you undertake to share all that the future may bring. All the sweetness life's cup may hold for you should be sweeter because you drink it together; whatever drops of bitterness it may contain should be less bitter because you share them.[1]

As I recite the blessing over the wine, we pray that God will bestow fullness of joy upon you.

בָּרוּךְ אַתָּה יְיָ אֱלֹהֵינוּ מֶלֶךְ הָעוֹלָם בּוֹרֵא פְּרִי הַגָּפֶן.

Blessed are you, (O Lord) our God, Creator of the fruit of the vine.

Selection 2

This cup of wine is symbolic of the cup of life. As you share this cup of wine, you undertake to share all the future may bring. May you find life's joys doubly gladdened, its bitterness sweetened, and all things hallowed by true companionship and love.[2]

Two cups are before you. By your choice, only one of the cups is reserved for the two of you alone. You decided to share the first cup with those who have been partners in your lives thus far, the ones who have helped to make you the individuals you are.

This cup of wine symbolizes the gratitude (bride) and (groom) have for the loving care and teaching of parents, the ties of heart and mind and memory that link brothers and sisters, and for the friendships that fill this cup to overflowing.[3]

בָּרוּךְ אַתָּה יְיָ אֱלֹהֵינוּ מֶלֶךְ הָעוֹלָם בּוֹרֵא פְּרִי הַגָּפֶן.

Blessed are you, O God, Creator of the fruit of the vine.

Selection 3

This cup of wine is symbolic of the cup of life. As you share this cup of wine, you undertake to share all that the future may bring.

בָּרוּךְ אַתָּה יְיָ אֱלֹהֵינוּ מֶלֶךְ הָעוֹלָם בּוֹרֵא פְּרִי הַגָּפֶן.

Blessed are you, O God, Creator of the fruit of the vine.

As together you have partaken from this cup of wine, so may you in union and devotion to one another draw contentment, comfort, and happiness from the cup of life. Thereby may you find life's joys doubly gladdened, its bitterness sweetened, and all things hallowed by true companionship and love.

Selection 4

(Bride) and (groom), this wine is a symbol of the sweetness we wish for your married life. There will be times when you drink from other cups, bitter ones, but life offers opportunity to savor the sweetness and joy of wine more often than the darkness of sorrow. And as you share in each

other's life, you will henceforth share all things. Symbolic of this cooperation, you will now share this cup of wine with each other and with
your parents.

בָּרוּךְ אַתָּה יְיָ אֱלֹהֵינוּ מֶלֶךְ הָעוֹלָם בּוֹרֵא פְּרִי הַגָּפֶן.

Blessed are you, O God, Creator of the fruit of the vine.

Selection 5

Two thoughts are suggested by this cup of wine. The first is that wine is a
symbol of the sweetness we wish for your life. There will be times when
you drink from other cups, bitter ones, but life more often offers opportunity to savor sweetness. The awareness of the possibility of a life filled
with true meaning is what we toast: the good that is life.[4]

The second is that wine is a symbol of sharing. You two have shared
many years together, and out of this time together has grown the love,
which brought you to this day. As you continue to share in each other's
life, you will, as a symbol of this enduring cooperation, share this cup
of wine.[5]

בָּרוּךְ אַתָּה יְיָ אֱלֹהֵינוּ מֶלֶךְ הָעוֹלָם בּוֹרֵא פְּרִי הַגָּפֶן.

Blessed are you, O God, Creator of the fruit of the vine.

Selection 6

The blessing over the wine, known as the kiddush, is a part of many
Jewish celebrations and holidays. The word *kiddush* means sanctification,
so as we recite this blessing, we symbolically sanctify this couple on their
wedding day.

בָּרוּךְ אַתָּה יְיָ אֱלֹהֵינוּ מֶלֶךְ הָעוֹלָם בּוֹרֵא פְּרִי הַגָּפֶן.

Blessed are you, O God, Creator of the fruit of the vine.

Circling

It is an old Jewish custom for the bride to circle the groom as part of the wedding ceremony. Traditionally, brides circle their groom either three or seven times. Seven circles symbolize the seven times the Bible states, "When a man takes a wife." The three circles correspond to the three times the phrase, "I will betroth thee unto me," appears in a passage from the Book of Hosea. Circles, in general, are also considered symbols of protection.

While this circling is a part of many Orthodox Jewish weddings, it is seldom included in a Reform or interfaith wedding. I mention the circling here because an increasing number of couples are choosing to use a new version of the circling in their ceremonies. Two such modern innovations appear below.

Selection 1
It is a very old Jewish folk custom for the bride to circle the groom during the wedding ceremony. The circle was believed to create an invisible wall of protection for them from evil spirits. The circle symbolized the new relationship of the bride and groom, each now becoming the center of the other's attention. Today, after reciting a beautiful marriage vow from the Book of Hosea, (bride) and (groom) will circle each other one time as a sign of respect for each other's individuality, as a symbol of their appreciation of their differences, which enrich their lives, and as a sign of their

love. As the Cabalists, or Jewish mystics, claim, this circling helps each of them enter the spheres of the other's soul.

[Before each circles around the other, they say the following:]

Bride and groom:
I shall betroth thee unto me forever,
Yea, I shall betroth thee unto me in righteousness,
And in lovingkindness and in compassion;
And I shall betroth thee unto me in faithfulness.

(Hosea 2:21–22)[1]

Selection 2
It is a very old Jewish custom for the bride to circle the groom three or seven times. Some believe you should circle three times based on a passage from the book of Hosea that repeats the phrase, "I will betroth you to me" three times. Others believe you should circle seven times. According to Jewish mystics, seven is a very powerful number. Circling seven times was thought to help the bride enter the seven mystical spheres of the groom's soul.

Today, brides and grooms are adding new meanings to this tradition. For their ceremony, (bride) and (groom) have chosen to circle each other (one, three, or seven) times, as a sign of the mutuality of their love, to symbolize their respect for their individuality, and to acknowledge the sacredness of this union of their lives.

Music may be played during the circling, or you may choose to have your officiant or friend read one of the following biblical passages or some other love poem or reading:

I will betroth you to me forever;
I will betroth you to me in righteousness and in justice, in
     steadfast love, and in mercy.
I will betroth you to me in faithfulness.

(Hosea 2:21–22)

Set me as a seal upon your heart,
    as a seal upon your arm;
Many waters cannot quench love,
    nor can floods drown it.
I am my beloved's and my beloved is mine.
(Song of Songs 8:6, 8:7, and 6:3)

Affirmation of the Families
and of the Guests

It is a Protestant custom to include an affirmation by the families and the guests as part of a wedding ceremony. This is the moment in the service where the priest or minister asks everyone present if they will pledge their support for the bride and groom in their married life together.

This is a nice way to acknowledge and honor your family and friends as important members of your community.

Selection 1
Officiant:
Will all of you who are family and friends of (bride) and (groom) affirm your continuing support and love of them in their marriage?

Family and friends:
We will.

Officiant:
Will you offer them your wisdom and encouragement in their times of struggle, and your celebration with them in their times of joy?

Family and friends:
We will.

Selection 2
Officiant:
(Names of parents and/or other family members), do you give your blessing to (bride) and (groom), and promise to do everything in your power to uphold them in their marriage?

Family and friends:
We do.

Officiant:
Will all of you witnessing these vows do everything in your power to uphold (bride) and (groom) in their marriage?

Family and friends:
We will.[1]

Selection 3
Officiant:
This marriage unites not only two individuals, but two families and two communities as well. I now ask you, (bride) and (groom)'s (grandparents, parents, brothers, sisters, extended family members and friends), do you promise to support (bride) and (groom) in their marriage?

All respond:
We do.

Vows

Wedding vows can vary greatly in style and content. Some are written in the form of a question, others in the form of a statement. Some speak in general terms about love and commitment; others are very personal statements that the bride and groom share with each other. In this chapter, you will see examples of all of these styles.

For your ceremony, choose the style that best suits your personality. If, for example, you are anxious about speaking in public, you may want your vows posed to you in the form of a question. When asked if you promise to love and cherish your partner, you simply respond with one word: "Yes!" If you are more comfortable speaking in front of your family and friends, you may prefer to write your own vows and recite them directly to each other. If this is the case, I recommend that you either repeat the words of your vows after your officiant or that you read your vows from index cards. I urge you not to rely totally on your memory for your vows. In almost twenty years of experience, I can count on one hand the number of brides and grooms who have been able to recite their vows totally from memory. Even those who are accomplished public speakers have difficulty saying these few sentences from memory without stumbling.

Remember, your vows are very personal and emotional words. It is not unusual for both brides and grooms to shed a few tears at this moment in their ceremony. If this happens to you, try not to panic or be embarrassed. I know from experience that most people, including me, find it touching if a bride and groom are so filled with emotion that they struggle to speak their vows. It is one sign of the depth of their caring and love for each other.

Selection 1
Do you, (groom/bride), take (bride/groom) to be your wife/husband, promising to cherish and protect her/him, whether in good fortune or in adversity, for all the days of your life?

Selection 2
And now I ask you, in the presence of God and this assembly: Do you, (groom/bride), take (bride/groom) to be your wife/husband, to love, to honor, and to cherish?

Selection 3
I, (bride/groom), take you, (groom/bride), to be my husband/wife, to have and to hold, to love and to cherish, to honor and to respect, forsaking all others. I, (bride/groom), promise to love you and care for you, in sickness and in health, for richer or for poorer, for better or for worse, from this day forward.

Selection 4
Groom:
I give to you my hand and my love. I will respect you, honor you, and live my life openly with you. Through my love for you, I pledge to work to increase your happiness and to diminish your sorrows. I promise to cherish and protect you in good fortune and in adversity from this day forward.

Selection 5
I, (groom), take you, (bride), to be my wife. I give you my hand and my heart. I pledge to share my life openly with you and to speak loving truth to you. I promise to respect and honor you, care for you in tenderness, support you with patience and love, and walk with you through all the seasons of our lives.[1]

Selection 6
Bride and groom:
I promise to love you, to respect you, to laugh with you, and to soothe your tears. I promise to share my life openly and honestly with you and to encourage and nurture your growth. Together, we continue this journey of exploration, trust, and communication. I promise to savor each day, reveling in our loving relationship and in our pursuit of happiness.[2]

Selection 7

> I, (bride), take you, (groom), to be no other than yourself
> loving what I know of you
> trusting what I do not yet know
> with respect for your integrity
> and faith in your love for me
> through all our years
> and in all that life may bring us.
>
> I promise to try to be ever open to you
> and above all, to do everything in my power
> to permit you to become the person you are yet to be.
> I give you my love.[3]

Selection 8
Officiant:
(Groom/bride) will you have (bride/groom) to be your wife/husband, to live together in the covenant of faith, hope, and love? Will you listen to her/his innermost thoughts, be considerate and tender in your care of her/him, and to stand by her/him faithfully in sickness and in health, and preferring her/him above all others, accept full responsibility for her/his every necessity as long as you both shall live?

Selection 9
Officiant:
(Bride) and (groom), now is the time to affirm your love and commitment by exchanging your vows and rings.

Bride:

We promise to love, honor, and cherish each other in times of hardship and in times of happiness, and we pledge our fidelity as a token of love and honor.

Groom:

In times of trouble we will try to be patient with each other and with ourselves. In times of joy, we will try to help each other experience happiness to the fullest.

Bride:

We hope that we will always be supportive of each other's values, and that we will help each other live a life of which we can be proud. We pledge to assess the direction of our lives at intervals and take care that our vocation, avocations, and way of life are consonant with our beliefs.

Groom:

We hope we will always maintain the ties of family and friendship. As a family we promise to treasure the old relationships with friends and family and we promise to welcome new ones. We promise to treat each other with respect and to listen to each other, especially when we do not like what we hear. And we promise to try to make our relationship a role model for future generations.

Bride and groom:

May God grant us the strength to keep all of the pledges we are making today.

Standing side by side, we will try to give each other the courage to reach for our highest aspirations.[4]

Selection 10
Officiant:

(Bride) and (groom), the union of husband and wife in heart, body, and mind is intended for their mutual joy; for the help and comfort given each other in prosperity and adversity, and the creation of a family. Therefore marriage is not to be entered into unadvisedly or lightly, but reverently and deliberately. With this in mind, I ask you to declare your intentions.

(Bride) and (groom), have you come here freely and without reservations to give yourselves to each other in marriage?

Bride and groom:
We have.

Officiant:
Will you love, comfort, honor, and keep each other, in sickness and in health, and be faithful to each other as long as you both shall live?

Bride and groom:
We will.

Officiant:
Will all of you who are family and friends of (bride) and (groom) affirm your continuing support and love of them in their marriage?

Family and friends:
We will.

Officiant:
Will you offer them your wisdom and encouragement in their times of struggle, and your celebration with them in their times of joy?

Family and friends:
We will.

Officiant:
(Bride) and (groom), since it is your intention to enter into marriage, join your right hands and repeat after me.

Groom:
In the name of God, I, (groom), take you, (bride), to be my wife, to have and to hold from this day forward, for better, for worse, for richer, for

poorer, in sickness and in health, to love and to cherish, until we are parted by death. This is my solemn vow.

Bride:
In the name of God, I, (bride), take you, (groom), to be my husband, to have and to hold from this day forward, for better, for worse, for richer, for poorer, in sickness and in health, to love and to cherish, until we are parted by death. This is my solemn vow.[5]

Selection 14: Declaration of Consent
Officiant:
Before God and your family and friends, I ask you to affirm your willingness to enter into this covenant of marriage and to share all the joys and sorrow of this new relationship, whatever the future may hold.

(Groom), will you have this woman to be your wife; to live together in the covenant of marriage? Will you love her, comfort her, honor and keep her, in sickness and in health; and forsaking all others, be faithful to her as long as you both shall live?

Groom:
I will.

Officiant:
(Bride), will you have this man to be your husband; to live together in the covenant of marriage? Will you love him, comfort him, honor and keep him, in sickness and in health; and forsaking all others, be faithful to him as long as you both shall live?

Bride:
I will.

Ring Exchanges

🎚

In this chapter, you will find several introductions to the exchange of rings, along with examples of words that you might say as you place your rings on each other's finger.

For your ceremony, choose one of the following or combine and edit different passages as you wish.

Selection 1

In keeping with the declaration you have made, you give and you receive these rings. They are tokens of your union, symbols of enduring loyalty. May they ever remind you that your lives are to be bound together by devotion and faithfulness.[1]

As you, (groom/bride), place this ring upon the finger of your bride/groom, speak to her/him these words:

הֲרֵי אַתְּ מְקוּדֶּשֶׁת (אַתָּה מְקֻדָּשׁ) לִי בְּטַבַּעַת זוֹ כְּדַת מֹשֶׁה וְיִשְׂרָאֵל.

By this ring you are consecrated (or sanctified) to me as my wife/husband in accordance with the traditions of Moses and Israel.[2]

Selection 2

The exchange of rings is central to the wedding ceremony. It is based on the marriage formula called the Haray Aht. The Haray Aht contains thirty-two letters. In Hebrew the number 32 is written with the letters lamed and bet, which spell the word *lev*, which means heart. Although (bride) and (groom) use slightly different words, they do so in the same spirit of this custom and thus symbolically give their hearts to one another as they recite these words.

(Groom/bride), repeat after me:

הֲרֵי אַתְּ מְקֻדֶּשֶׁת (אַתָּה מְקֻדָּשׁ) לִי בְּטַבַּעַת זוֹ לְפִי אֱמוּנָתֵינוּ.

By this ring you are consecrated (or sanctified) to me as my wife/husband in accordance with our beliefs.

Selection 3

These rings in their unbroken wholeness are tokens of your union and of your love. They are symbols of the enduring trust and affection that you bring to one another. May they ever remind you that your lives are to be bound together by devotion and faithfulness.[3]

Groom/bride:

הֲרֵי אַתְּ מְקֻדֶּשֶׁת (אַתָּה מְקֻדָּשׁ) לִי בְּטַבַּעַת זוֹ בְּעֵינֵי יְיָ.

Be consecrated to me as my wife/husband in the eyes of God.

With this ring I join my life with yours.

אֲנִי לְדוֹדִי וְדוֹדִי לִי.

I am my beloved's and my beloved is mine.

Selection 4

These rings in their unbroken wholeness are tokens of your union and of your love. They represent the enduring trust and affection that you bring to one another, and are the outward and visible symbols of an inner spiritual bond.

(Groom/bride), please repeat after me:

I join my life with yours in loving kindness and compassion.
I join my life with yours in faithfulness.

[Place the ring.]

This is my beloved and this is my friend.

Selection 5

We have all witnessed your exchange of vows. Yet, words are fleeting, and the sound of them will soon be gone. Therefore, the wedding rings become enduring symbols of the promises you have made to each other. The wedding rings are regarded as fitting symbols of marriage, for they are fashioned to have neither beginning nor end. The wedding rings are outward and visible symbols of your inner spiritual bond.

(Groom/bride), repeat after me:
I join my life with yours and offer myself into your loving care.

[Place the ring on your partner's finger.]

You are my beloved and you are my friend.

Selection 6

As by these rings you symbolize your marriage bond, may their meaning sink into your hearts and bind your lives together by dedication and faithfulness to each other. Truly, then, will these rings celebrate the words of the Song of Songs:

> Wear me as a seal upon your heart,
> As a seal upon your arm;
> For love is infinitely strong . . .
> Many waters cannot quench love;
> No flood can sweep it away . . .
>
> (Song of Songs 8:6 and 8:7)

Selection 7

These rings are visible symbols of your inner spiritual bond. As you, (groom/bride), place this ring on (bride/groom)'s finger, repeat after me:

I give you this ring as a symbol of my commitment to you and to our partnership in life. You have my heart always.[4]

Selection 8

Lord, bless these rings that we bless in your name. Grant that those who wear them always have a deep faith in each other. May they do your will and always live together in peace, good will, and love.[5]

May these rings in their unbroken wholeness be tokens of the continuity of your love. And may their shining substance be a symbol of the enduring trust and affection that you bring to one another.[6]

(Groom), repeat after me: With this ring, I thee wed.

(Bride), repeat after me: With this ring, I thee wed.

The Unity Candle

Many interfaith wedding ceremonies include the lighting of a unity candle. This is a visual symbol of two lives joining together as one in the new union of marriage. Although this custom is associated with Christian weddings, it has no apparent religious origins. One priest I know calls the unity candle a Hallmark invention. But, regardless of its beginning, it is still a nice ritual.

In this section, you will see different approaches to the unity candle, including one that combines both Jewish and Christian sources.

Selection 1
In the wedding liturgy, candlelight symbolizes the commitment of love these two people are declaring today.

Before you, you see three special candles. The two smaller candles symbolize the lives of the bride and groom. Until today, both have let their light shine as individuals in their respective communities. Now they have come to publicly proclaim their love in the new union of marriage.

They do not lose their individuality. Yet, in marriage, they are united in so close a bond that they become one. Now, following the profession of their marriage vows, they will light the large center candle from the smaller candles to symbolize this new reality. In this way they are saying that henceforth their light must shine together for each other, for their families, and for the community.[1]

Selection 2

> *[The couple lights one large candle*
> *as these words are recited:]*

From every human being there rises a light that reaches straight to heaven. And when two souls are destined to find each other, their two streams of light flow together and a single brighter light goes forth from their united being.

(Baal Shem Tov)

Selection 3

> *Family member:*

בָּרוּךְ אַתָּה יְיָ בּוֹרֵא מְאוֹרֵי הָאֵשׁ שֶׁל הַשִּׂמְחָה שֶׁלָּנוּ.

Blessed are you, O God, Creator of the light of celebration.

בָּרוּךְ אַתָּה יְיָ אֱלֹהֵינוּ מֶלֶךְ הָעוֹלָם שֶׁהֶחֱיָנוּ וְקִיְּמָנוּ וְהִגִּיעָנוּ לַזְּמַן הַזֶּה.

We praise you, O God, Ruler of the universe, who has given us life, sustained us, and brought us to this joyous time.

> *[The couple lights the large candle.]*

Officiant:
From every human being there rises a light that reaches straight to heaven. And when two souls are destined to find each other, their two streams of light flow together and a single brighter light goes forth from their united being.

(Baal Shem Tov)

Selection 4
Rabbi:
In the wedding liturgy, candlelight symbolizes the commitment of love these two people have declared today.

Before you, you see three special candles. The two smaller candles symbolize the lives of the bride and groom. Until today, both have let their light shine as individuals in their respective communities. Now they publicly proclaim their love in the new union of marriage. They light the large center candle from the smaller candles to symbolize this new reality.

[Bride and groom light the havdalah candle.]

This center candle is a multiwicked, braided candle known as a havdalah candle. It is traditionally used as part of a Jewish ritual that ends the Sabbath on Saturday night. Today, however, we are using it for a different purpose, to symbolize the intertwining of the lives of the bride and groom. The flame of this candle also burns larger and brighter than any individual candle. The symbolism of this candle is reflected in this quote from the Baal Shem Tov, a mystical rabbi who lived centuries ago: From every human being there rises a light that reaches straight to heaven. And when two souls are destined to find one another, their two streams of light flow together and a single brighter light goes forth from their united being.

Selection 5
Officiant:
The connection between the flame and the human spirit as symbolized by the candle lighting is well stated in the reading, "The World," by Eduardo Galeano, translated by Cedric Belfrage as follows:[2]

A man from a town of Negua, on the coast of Colombia, could climb into the sky. On his return, he described his trip. He told how he had contemplated human life from on high. He said we are a sea of tiny flames. Each person shines with his or her own light. No two flames are alike. There are big flames and little flames, flames of every color. Some people's flames are so still they don't even flicker in the wind while others have wild flames that fill the air with sparks. Some foolish flames neither burn nor shed light, but blaze with life so fiercely that you can't look at them without blinking and if you approach, you shine in fire.

[Bride/groom light the candle.]

As the one light cannot be divided, neither shall their lives be divided, but always bear witness to the unity and harmony of their home.[3]

The Ketubah Signing
and Reading

While most couples sign their interfaith ketubah immediately before their ceremony, some choose to read and sign the document as a part of their service (see "The Interfaith Ketubah" in Part I).

If you decide to sign your ketubah during your ceremony, you may wish to explain and introduce the ritual with one of the following passages:

Selection 1
Rabbi:
It is a Jewish custom to sign a ketubah, or wedding contract, as part of the wedding rituals. Originally it was a legal document that spelled out some of the rights and obligations of the couple in marriage. Today, most ketubot (plural form of ketubah) are spiritual, not legal, covenants that the bride and groom make with one another.

The ketubah is traditionally signed before the ceremony, but (bride) and (groom) chose to sign it as part of their service, so that all of you could hear the words and witness the signing. I would like to read it to you now.

Selection 2
Rabbi:
The ketubah, or Jewish wedding contract, will now be signed by (bride) and (groom) and two nonrelated witnesses that they have chosen to confirm their marriage. The ketubah, traditionally presented to the bride

from the groom prior to the ceremony, was originally instituted to legalize the husband's obligations to her. Today, however, it is more of a spiritual covenant that the couple makes with each other. Since all of you here mean so much to (bride) and (groom), they have chosen to enter into this agreement in your company.

The Seven Jewish
Wedding Blessings

The seven Jewish wedding blessings are included in many but not all interfaith wedding ceremonies. If you wish to include them, you may select one of the several variations in this section. They range from Hebrew translations and interpretations to entirely new sets of contemporary blessings. Perhaps you would like to try writing seven of your own!

If you choose one of the more traditional versions, you also have the option of including the Hebrew as well as the English. If you do include the Hebrew, I strongly recommend that you alternate reciting the English and Hebrew of each blessing. This will keep the service flowing. See the sample ceremonies in Part II for examples, and see Appendix III for the Hebrew and transliterations for the traditional seven blessings.

I have also included a few options for introducing these blessings.

Introductions

Selection 1
Historically, brides and grooms have been blessed with seven wedding blessings. The first six praise God for creating the world, man and woman, children, peace and harmony, and the joys of marriage. The seventh, the blessing over the wine, symbolically sanctifies this day and this marriage.

I bless you now with these blessings (or an interpretation of these blessings).

Selection 2
Historically, brides and grooms have been blessed with seven wedding blessings. In Jewish mysticism, the number seven symbolizes creation and completion. As a man and woman join together in love and marriage, they help each other feel more complete, more whole than they ever felt alone. For their ceremony, (bride) and (groom) have chosen these seven contemporary blessings that reflect their own hopes and feelings for each other.

Selection 3
Historically, brides and grooms have been blessed with seven wedding blessings. The number seven is very powerful in Jewish mysticism. According to the Bible, God created the world in seven days; and marriage is a seven-day-a-week creation. As a man and woman join together in love, they make each other feel more complete and whole. For their ceremony, (bride) and (groom) have chosen to write six of their own blessings, blessings that reflect important values that give their lives meaning. The seventh blessing, the blessing over the wine, symbolically sanctifies this day and this marriage.[1]

Selection 4
In Judaism, seven is a significant number. According to Torah, the Jewish Bible, the physical world was created in six days. The seventh day created rest, peace, and a taste of paradise. A marriage may not be created in seven days, but it may represent a taste of paradise. Every marriage is a creative process. It is the creation of a family, an ever-growing, unfolding process of love and understanding, a creation born out of a couple's love for one another.

Each Jewish marriage is sanctified by seven blessings. They echo the path of creation. The first blessing celebrates the Creator's ability to create. Each blessing then becomes more specific, giving thanks for the creation of man and woman, then the birth of children, and the joys of marriage. These seven blessings, known in Hebrew as the Sheva Berachot, call marriage a joyful time that each generation should know. They include a blessing over the wine. All Jewish contracts, including marriage, becomes binding when sealed by the kiddush. This blesses the creation of a new family.[2]

The Seven Wedding Blessings

Selection 1

We praise you, Adonai our God, Ruler of the universe, Creator of the fruit of the vine.

We praise you, Adonai our God, Ruler of the universe, Creator of all things for your glory.

We praise you, Adonai our God, Ruler of the universe, Creator of man and woman.

We praise you, Adonai our God, Ruler of the universe, who creates us to share with you in life's everlasting renewal.

We praise you, Adonai our God, who causes Zion to rejoice in her children's happy return.

We praise you, Adonai our God, who causes bride and groom to rejoice. May these loving companions rejoice as have your creatures since the days of creation.

We praise you, Adonai our God, Ruler of the universe, Creator of joy and gladness, bride and groom, love and kinship, peace and friendship. O God, may there always be heard in the cities of Israel and in the streets of Jerusalem: the sounds of joy and of happiness, the voice of the groom and the voice of the bride, the shouts of young people celebrating, and the songs of children at play. We praise You, our God, who causes the bride and groom to rejoice together.[3]

Selection 2

Holy One of Blessing, your Presence fills creation, as all creation reflects your splendor.

Holy One of Blessing, your Presence fills creation, giving life to each human being.

Holy One of Blessing, your Presence fills creation. You created man and woman in your image, each reflecting the image of God forever. Holy One of Blessing, you give life to every being.

How happy is she who thought herself childless and then finds that her children gather to rejoice within her. Holy One of Blessing, you make Zion happy with her children.

May these cherished friends rejoice in joy as you once rejoiced in your creation of the Garden of Eden. Holy One of Blessing, your Presence radiates joy for the bride and groom.

Holy One of Blessing, your Presence fills creation. You created joy and gladness, bridegroom and bride, delight, song, laughter and gaiety, love and harmony, peace and friendship. May all Israel soon ring with voices of gladness and joy, voices of bridegrooms and brides, voices raised in joyful wedding celebrations, voices lifted in festive singing. Holy One of Blessing, your Presence radiates for the bride and groom.

Holy One of Blessing, your Presence fills creation, forming the fruit of the vine.[4]

Selection 3
Blessed is the Holy One, provider of all things, bringing forth the fruit of the vine, symbol of our sustenance and our rejoicing.

Praise and thanks, O Lord our God, Source of all creation, we stand in awe. We cannot know your name, yet each separate moment and every distinct object points to and shares in your Being.

Praise and thanks, O Lord our God, you have sanctified us in holiness. May we come to embody the divine attributes already at our core, in our thoughts and actions toward other humans and sentient beings.

Blessed is the Holy Spirit. May (bride) and (groom) find wonder as two people joined together to live as one.

Praise and thanks, Sovereign beyond divinity, may all who wander find homes, and may this joyous gathering be blessed.

Praise and thanks, Sovereign of all energy, we call forth an abundance of love to envelop these two people. May they be for each other lovers and friends, and may they each find fulfillment in life.

Blessed is the Holy One. May there come a day when the dominant force in the world will be the voices of lovers, the play of children, the happy sounds of feasting and singing.[5]

Selection 4
We acknowledge the Unity of all within the sovereignty of God, expressing our appreciation for this wine, symbol of our rejoicing.

We acknowledge the Unity of all within the sovereignty of God, realizing that each separate moment and every distinct object points to and shares in this oneness.

We acknowledge the Unity of all within the sovereignty of God, recognizing and appreciating the blessing of being human.

We acknowledge the Unity of all within the sovereignty of God, realizing the special gift of awareness that permits us to perceive this unity, and the wonder we experience as a man and a woman join to live together.

May rejoicing resound throughout the world as the homeless are given homes, persecution and oppression cease, and all people learn to live in peace with each other and in harmony with their environment.

From the source of all energy we call forth an abundance of love to envelop this couple. May they be for each other lovers and friends, and may their love partake of the same innocence, purity, and sense of discovery that we imagine the first couple to have experienced.

We acknowledge the Unity of all, and we highlight today joy and gladness, bridegroom and bride, delight and cheer, love and harmony, peace and companionship. May we all witness the day when the dominant sounds in Jerusalem and throughout the world will be these sounds of happiness, the voices of lovers, the sounds of feasting and singing. Praised is love; blessed be this marriage. May the bride and bridegroom rejoice together.[6]

Selection 5
Blessed is the creation that embodies glory.

Blessed is the creation of the human being.

Blessed is the design of the human being, united in heart and the search for love.

Blessed is the joy of our gathering. May rejoicing resound throughout the world as the homeless are given homes, persecution and oppression cease, and all people learn to live in peace with each other and in harmony with their environment.

Let these loving friends rejoice. May their joy be as paradise on earth.

Blessed is the creation of joy and celebration, bride and groom, delight and cheer, love and solidarity, peace and companionship. Praised is love, blessed be this marriage.

This cup of wine is symbolic of the cup of life, a life enriched by family and friends who have nurtured you and helped you become the individuals you are today. As you share this cup of wine, you undertake to share all that future may bring. All the sweetness life's cup may hold for you should be sweeter because you drink it together; whatever drops of bitterness it may contain should be less bitter because you share them.

בָּרוּךְ אַתָּה יְיָ אֱלֹהֵינוּ מֶלֶךְ הָעוֹלָם בּוֹרֵא פְּרִי הַגָּפֶן.

Blessed is the creation of the fruit of the vine.[7]

Selection 6

Blessed is the creation of the fruit of the vine.

Blessed is the creation which embodies glory.

Blessed is the creation of the human being.

Blessed is the design of the human being. Developing our wisdom we may become Godlike. We are assembled from the very fabric of the universe and we are composed of eternal elements. Blessed be and blessed is our creation.

Rejoice and be glad you who wandered homeless. In joy have you gathered with your sisters and your brothers. Blessed is the joy of our gathering.

Bestow happiness on these loving mates as would creatures feel in Eden's garden. Blessed be the joy of lovers.

Blessed is the creation of joy and celebration, lover and mate, gladness and jubilation, pleasure and delight, love and solidarity, friendship and peace. Soon may we hear in the streets of the city and the paths of the fields, the voice of joy, the voice of gladness, the voice of lover, the voice of mate, the triumphant voice of lovers from the canopy and the voice of youths from their feasts of song. Blessed Blessed Blessed is the joy of lovers, one with each other.[8]

Selection 7

Blessed are you, Lord God, who created life.

Blessed are you, Lord God, who created man and woman.

Blessed are you, Lord God, who unites man and woman.

Bless these two who stand before you as you blessed the first couple in the Garden of Eden.

Blessed are you, Lord God, who grants the joy of marriage.

May we all see the day when the world will echo with the sounds of feasting and singing. Praised is love; blessed be this union.

This cup of wine is symbolic of the cup of life. As you share the one cup of wine, you undertake to share all that the future may bring. All the sweetness life's cup may hold for you should be sweeter because you drink it together; whatever drops of bitterness it may contain should be less bitter because you share them.[9]

As I recite the blessing over the wine, we pray that God will bestow fullness of joy upon you.

בָּרוּךְ אַתָּה יְיָ אֱלֹהֵינוּ מֶלֶךְ הָעוֹלָם בּוֹרֵא פְּרִי הַגָּפֶן.

> Blessed are you, Lord God of the universe, who created the fruit of the vine.

Selection 8
Cherished be the earth, the provider of all things.

Cherished be the hopes and aspirations of friends and family.

May we respect the diversity of humankind.

May we acknowledge the cyclical nature of life.

May we acknowledge the human need for providing a home.

Honored be the tradition of bride and groom and their happiness at this rite of passage that is celebrated the world over.

Praised be the sounds of joy and happiness, the voice of the groom and the voice of the bride, the shouts of young people celebrating, and the songs of children at play. We praise the bride and groom rejoicing together.

Selection 9
May your marriage enrich your lives.

May you work together to build a relationship of substance and quality.

May the honesty of your communication build a foundation of understanding, connection and trust.

May you respect each other's individual personality and philosophy, and give each other room to grow and fulfill each other's dreams.

May your sense of humor and playful spirit continue to enliven your relationship.

May you understand that neither of you is perfect: you are both subject to human frailties; and may your love strengthen when you fall short of each other's expectations.

May you be "best friends," better together than either of you are apart.[10]

Selection 10: Seven Blessings from Seven Different Traditions
Jewish-Yiddish
May God be very good to you and bless you with much happiness, many good years together with beautiful children and grandchildren. May I live to see it all and have a lot of *nachas*[11] in you.[12]

Christian
Holy Father, Creator of the Universe, maker of man and woman in your likeness, source of blessing for married life, we humbly pray to You for (bride) and (groom) who today are united in this sacrament of marriage. May Your fullest blessing come upon them so that they may together rejoice in Your gift of married love. (Bride) and (groom), may you reach old age in the company of your friends, and come at last to the kingdom of heaven.

Russian
May you have one hundred years of happiness together.

Irish
May the road rise up to meet you,
May the wind always be at your back,
May the sun shine warm upon your face,
May the rain fall freely on your fields, and
May God hold you in the palm of his hand.

Italian
There are three beautiful things in life: birth, love, and this day. Best wishes and good fortune to you, (bride) and (groom), for all of your life.

Chinese
May your two hearts and two souls be united for one hundred years of eternity.

Wampanoag Indian
May the Great Spirit protect you, keep you together, and sustain your love for Mother Earth.[13]

Selection 11
Blessing for the Earth, Environment, and Nature
Nature and the environment provide sustenance for our bodies and spirit. Land, air, water, all living creatures and plants bring us great joy. Our appreciation of nature reveals an essence of ourselves.

Blessing for the Diversity of Humankind
The recognition of differences in each other as well as the recognition of the things we have in common helps us to appreciate the diversity and commonality we find in all humankind. We are challenged to respect each other for those differences. We learn tolerance through our relationship and the understanding of difference makes our lives richer.

Blessing for Peace and Freedom for All People
We are fortunate to live our lives in peace and freedom and we wish for a world free from suffering and oppression. May the actions we take in our lives contribute to the making of a better world.

Blessed Is the Joy of Art and Music
We are blessed with art and music. They add joy and fulfillment to our lives. Through the making of art we become in touch with ourselves, through the sharing of art we are brought closer to each other and to our fellow human beings.

Blessing for Family and Friends
We are grateful for the love and support of our parents, families, and friends, love that is expressed in laughter and through tears, and support that is founded on trust and respect. We wish good health, long life, and much happiness for all those we love.

Blessing for Bride and Groom
Bless (bride) and (groom) in their life and home together.

Blessing over the Wine

בָּרוּךְ אַתָּה יְיָ אֱלֹהֵינוּ מֶלֶךְ הָעוֹלָם בּוֹרֵא פְּרִי הַגָּפֶן.

Blessed are you, Adonai our God, Ruler of the universe, Creator of the fruit of the vine.[14]

Selection 12
May you be generous and giving with each other.

May your sense of humor and playful spirit always continue to enliven your relationship.

May you always respect the diversity of humankind.

May you act with compassion to those less fortunate and with responsibility to the communities of which you are a part.

May you appreciate and complement each other's differences.

May you always share yourselves openly with your friends and family.

May your home be a haven of blessing and peace.[15]

Pronouncement

States do not require clergy, justices of the peace, or any officiant to recite a certain phrase or formula in order to validate a couple's marriage. You may choose any words you like for your pronouncement. Some couples like the tradition of being pronounced husband and wife according to the laws of the state in which they are getting married. Others prefer to emphasize their own love and commitment as the power that binds them together. For your ceremony, choose one of the following, or write your own pronouncement.

Selection 1
In the presence of this company as witness you have spoken the words and performed the rites that unite your lives. I, therefore, declare you, (groom) and (bride), husband and wife, married in accordance with the laws of the state of (name of state in which the marriage is being held) and according to your traditions.

[Bride and groom kiss.]

Selection 2
In the presence of these witnesses, you have spoken the words and performed the rites that unite your lives.

(Groom) and (bride), you are now husband and wife in the sight of God, your family and friends, and your community.

I ask you and all who are gathered here to pray in silence, seeking God's blessings upon your union and your home.

[Bride and groom kiss.]

Selection 3

Your friends and family, all of us here, rejoice in your happiness and we pray that this day marks only one of many more blessings you will share in the days and years ahead. And now that you have spoken the words and performed the rites that unite your lives, I do hereby, in accordance with your beliefs and the laws of this state, declare your marriage to be valid and binding, and I now declare you, (groom) and (bride), husband and wife.

[Bride and groom kiss.]

Selection 4

Now, by the power of your love, and the commitment you have made, you are husband and wife.

[Bride and groom kiss.]

Selection 5

(Groom) and (bride), you are now husband and wife. Go now and live together as heirs of the grace of life.

[Bride and groom kiss.]

Selection 6

Your friends and family, all of us here, rejoice in your happiness and we pray that this day marks only one of many more blessings you will share in the days and years ahead. And now that you have spoken the words and performed the rites that unite your lives, we now, by the power of your love and the commitment you have made, declare your marriage to be valid and binding, and declare you, (groom) and (bride), husband and wife.

[Bride and groom kiss.]

Selection 7
Now that (groom) and (bride) have given themselves to each other by solemn vows, with the joining of hands and the giving and receiving of a ring, we pronounce them husband and wife in the name of God. Those whom God has joined together, let no one put asunder. Amen.

[Bride and groom kiss.]

Closing Prayers and Readings

❦

Before the final breaking of the glass, many interfaith couples conclude their ceremony with a traditional prayer known as the "priestly benediction." Since this biblical prayer is a familiar part of both Christian and Jewish liturgies, it provides a nice way to end the ceremony on a common religious note.

Of course, there are many other closing prayers and blessings that you may prefer to use in your ceremony. This section provides you with many choices from a variety of cultures and traditions. If you like, you may include two of these passages in your service. A few of the couples I have married included both the "priestly benediction" and one other closing reading that appealed to them.

Selection 1

יְבָרֶכְךָ יְיָ וְיִשְׁמְרֶךָ׃

May God bless you and keep you.

יָאֵר יְיָ פָּנָיו אֵלֶיךָ וִיחֻנֶּךָ׃

May God's countenance shine upon you and be gracious to you.

יִשָּׂא יְיָ פָּנָיו אֵלֶיךָ וְיָשֵׂם לְךָ שָׁלוֹם׃

May God look upon you with favor and grant you peace.
(Priestly Benediction, Numbers 6:24–26)

Selection 2

יִהְיֶה דַרְכְּךָ מְבוֹרָךְ.

May your way be blessed.

יָאֵר אֵלֶיךָ אוֹר הַחָכְמָה.

May wisdom's light shine upon you.

יָבִיאוּ לְךָ מַסָּעֲךָ שָׁלוֹם.

May your journey bring you peace.
(Modern benediction)

Selection 3

May the road rise up to greet you.
May the wind be always at your back.
May the sun shine warm upon your face.
And until we meet again
May God hold you in the hollow of his hand.
(Irish poem)

Selection 4

Now it is completed
The marriage ceremony,
Just like the moon descending
In its dazzling radiance.
The couple is given the happiness
Of those who watch
Which showers down upon them like gold.

This is the symbol,
The marriage ceremony,
With the blessings of all the guests,
That this marriage may be free from all misfortune
And bear eternal happiness forever.

(Javanese poem)

Selection 5

Now you will feel no rain,
    for each of you will be shelter for the other.
Now you feel no cold,
    for each of you will be warmth to the other,
Now there is no more loneliness,
    for each of you will be companion to the other.
Now you are two persons,
    but there is only one life before you.
Go now to your dwelling to enter into
    the days of your togetherness.
And may your days be good,
    and long upon the earth.

(Apache marriage poem)

Selection 6

May the courage of the early morning's dawning
And the strength of the eternal hills at noontime
And the peace of the open spaces at evening's ending
And the love that abides in your hearts, now and forever,
Bring you deep happiness.

(Javanese poem)

Selection 7

The wedding is not over, it is just begun. Not once and forever, but again and again shall the mystery of two people, together and in love, move one another and touch the world. For marriage is not something said and done, but a promise, whose fulfillment is acted out in time. Truth remains elusive, death a secret, love a challenge; life goes on neither more nor less incidentally than before, but one's hand is strengthened, one's way, brightened, and one's load, if not lightened, is made easier to bear.[1]

Selection 8

Eternal God, creator and preserver of all life, author of salvation, and giver of all grace: Look with favor upon the world you have made, (and for which your Son gave his life), and especially upon this man and this woman whom you make one flesh in holy matrimony.

Give them wisdom and devotion in the ordering of their common life, that each may be to the other a strength in need, a counselor in perplexity, a comfort in sorrow, and a companion in joy.

Grant that their wills may be so knit together in your will, and their spirits in your Spirit, that they may grow in love and peace with you and one another all the days of their lives.

Give them grace, when they hurt each other, to recognize and acknowledge their fault, and to seek each other's forgiveness and yours.

Make their life together a sign of God's (Christ's) love to this sinful and broken world, that unity may overcome estrangement, forgiveness heal guilt, and joy conquer despair. Amen.

Bestow on them, if it is your will, the gift and heritage of children, and the grace to bring them up to know you, to love you and to serve you.

Give them such fulfillment of their mutual affection that they may reach out in love and concern for others.

Grant that all married persons who have witnessed these vows may find their lives strengthened and their loyalties confirmed. . . .[2]

Selection 9

May both of you, now married, keep this covenant which you have made.

May you be a blessing and a comfort to each other, sharers of each other's joys, consolers of each other's sorrows, helpers to each other in the challenges of life.

May you encourage each other in whatever you set out to achieve.

May both of you, trusting each other, trust life and not be afraid.

May you not only express and accept affection between yourselves, but also reach out with love to all people.

We hope that the inspiration of this hour will not be forgotten. May you continue to love one another forever.[3]

Selection 10

    Deep Peace of the running wave to you.
    Deep Peace of the flowing air to you.
    Deep Peace of the quiet earth to you.
    Deep Peace of the shining stars to you.
    Deep Peace of the spirit of peace to you.

                       (Gaelic blessing)

The Yichud

If you plan to have a yichud following your wedding ceremony, I suggest that you explain the ritual to your guests during your service. This will help your guests appreciate another aspect of your ceremony.

I also suggest that you place the explanation here, before the breaking of the glass. After the glass is broken, it will be too difficult to get everyone's attention.

Selection 1
I would like to take this opportunity to mention to you, the guests, that (bride) and (groom) will be spending a few moments alone together, immediately following the ceremony. This is a custom called Yichud, which means union in Hebrew. It gives the couple an opportunity to share, privately, the power and importance of this moment in their lives. They will return shortly to greet you.

Selection 2
I would like to take this opportunity to mention to you, the guests, that (bride) and (groom) will be spending a few moments alone together immediately following the ceremony. This custom, known as Yichud in Hebrew, gives (bride) and (groom) a private moment to share their joy. It is here, in the privacy of the Yichud, that they will also share their first food and drink as husband and wife. After their Yichud, (bride) and (groom) will return to greet you and to join you in the wedding celebration.

Breaking of the Glass

❦

You may use one or more of the following explanations of the breaking of the glass in your wedding ceremony. As you will see in these passages, the breaking of the glass has acquired many new meanings over the last few years. One of these new interpretations explains that the breaking of the glass symbolizes the shattering of barriers between people of different cultures and faiths, quite an appropriate and powerful innovation for an interfaith ceremony!

In this section, you will find both traditional and modern interpretations of the breaking of the glass. You may choose one or a combination of them for your own ceremony.

Selection 1
We end the ceremony with the breaking of a glass. It is a very old custom, at least as old as the writing of the Talmud, or Jewish law, which was written around 500 C.E. The Talmud records that "Mar bar Rabina made a marriage feast for his son. He observed that the rabbis present were very happy. So he seized an expensive goblet worth four hundred zuzim and broke it before them. Thus he made them sober." His point was that rejoicing should be accompanied by an awareness of the seriousness of the occasion.

There are now many explanations for this custom. According to Orthodox Jewish beliefs, the breaking of the glass recalls the destruction of the ancient Temple, and it reminds us of our people's grief, even at a moment of great personal joy.

According to others, the broken glass reminds us that the world is still in exile, still broken, and that we have a responsibility to help mend it.

And to some, the breaking of the glass reminds us that marriage is a transforming experience, one that leaves the couple forever changed.

As (groom, or bride and groom) break(s) the glass(es), I invite everyone to shout "Mazel Tov," which means "Congratulations" and "Good Luck."

Selection 2

The traditional breaking of the glass marks the end of the ceremony and the beginning of the celebration.

As (groom, or bride and groom) break(s) the glass(es), I invite everyone to shout "Mazel Tov," which means "Congratulations" and "Good Luck."

Selection 3

The traditional breaking of the glass is a joyous ceremony. The fragility of the glass suggests the frailty of human relationships. The glass is broken to protect this marriage with the implied prayer: "As this glass shatters, so may your marriage never break."

As (groom, or bride and groom) break(s) the glass(es), I invite everyone to shout "Mazel Tov," which means "Congratulations" and "Good Luck."

Selection 4

It is a Jewish custom to end the wedding ceremony with the breaking of a glass. We don't know the exact origins of the custom. Some believe it has its roots in superstition, when people broke glasses to scare away evil spirits from such lucky people as brides and grooms. Whatever its beginnings, the breaking of the glass now has many interpretations, one of which says that even in the moment of our greatest joy, we should remember that there is still pain and suffering in the world, and that we have a responsibility to help relieve that pain and suffering. Another more common and joyous explanation says that we break the glass to mark the beginning of the celebration.

As (groom, or bride and groom) break(s) the glass(es), I invite everyone to shout "Mazel Tov," which means "Congratulations" and "Good Luck."

Selection 5

Although this wedding provides us with a taste of the joys and strengths of humanity, we break this glass to remind us that the world is still in exile, broken and requiring our care. Yet with all its broken dreams, it is still a beautiful world.[1]

Selection 6

Whatever its beginnings, the breaking of the glass now has many explanations and interpretations, including one that says that the breaking of the glass symbolizes the irrevocable change in the lives of the couple standing under the huppah. Marriage is a transforming experience, one that leaves the individuals forever changed. As the glass breaks, we begin the celebration.

Selection 7

The traditional breaking of the glass is a joyous ceremony. The fragility of the glass suggests the frailty of human relationships. The glass is broken to protect this marriage with the implied prayer: "May your bond of love be as difficult to break as it would be to put together the pieces of this glass."

Selection 8

We conclude the ceremony with the breaking of the glass. The breaking of the glass is irrevocable and permanent. So, too, may your marriage endure.

Selection 9

We end the ceremony with the traditional breaking of the glass. (Groom) or (bride and groom) will break this second cup of wine that we used to sanctify this marriage.

[Pour remaining wine in a bowl.]

Breaking this glass symbolizes the permanent change this marriage makes in (bride) and (groom)'s lives.

As (groom, or bride and groom) break(s) the glass, I invite everyone to shout "Mazel Tov," which means "Congratulations" and "Good Luck."

Selection 10

We end the ceremony with the breaking of this glass. Traditionally it marks the beginning of the wedding celebration. For (bride) and (groom), the shattering of this glass also symbolizes the breaking down of barriers between people of different cultures and faiths. May the day soon arrive when all people will live together in peace.

As (groom, or bride and groom) break(s) the glass, I invite everyone to shout "Mazel Tov," which means "Congratulations" and "Good Luck."

· PART IV ·

Wedding Readings

This collection of biblical and secular poetry and prose contains passages and poems that are frequently used in wedding ceremonies. You may choose one or more of them for your ceremony, or you may wish to include readings from other sources.

If you want to include some poetry and prose in your service, but you do not like what you find in these pages, I recommend three books that collectively contain hundreds of other possibilities. They are *Into the Garden: A Wedding Anthology*, edited by Robert Hass and Stephen Mitchell; *Wedding Readings*, selected by Eleanor Munro; and *The Book of Love*, edited by Diane Ackerman and Jeanne Mackin.

As mentioned earlier, you can place your readings anywhere in your service. See the sample ceremonies in Part II for ideas about placement.

Torah, or Hebrew Scripture, Passages

Selection 1

. . . wherever you go, I will go; wherever you lodge, I will lodge; your people shall be my people, and your God my God.

(Ruth 1:16)

Selection 2

And I shall betroth thee unto me forever,
Yea, I shall betroth thee unto me in righteousness,
And in loving kindness and in compassion;
And I shall betroth thee unto me in faithfulness.

(Hosea 2:19)

Selection 3

Wear me as a seal upon your heart
As a seal upon your arm;
For love is infinitely strong . . .
Many waters cannot quench love;
No flood can sweep it away.

(Song of Songs 8:6)[1]

Selection 4

Come, my beloved,
　　　let us go out into the fields
　　　and lodge in the villages.

Let us go early to the vineyards
>   and see whether the vines have budded,
>   whether the grape blossoms have opened
>   and the pomegranates are in full bloom.
>   There I will give you my love.

The mandrakes give forth their fragrance,
>   and at our doors are all choice fruits,
>   both fresh-picked and long-stored,
>   Have I kept, my beloved, for you.

(Song of Songs 7:12–14)

Selection 5

>   You have captured my heart,
>   My own, my bride,
>   You have captured my heart
>   with one glance of your eyes . . .

(Song of Songs 4:9)[2]

Selection 6

For everything there is a season, and a time for every matter under heaven:

>   a time to be born, and a time to die;
>   a time to plant, and a time to pluck up what is planted;
>   a time to break down, and a time to build up;
>   a time to weep, and a time to laugh;
>   a time to cast away stones, and a time to gather stones
>   together;
>   a time to embrace, and a time to refrain from embracing;
>   a time to seek, and a time to lose;
>   a time to keep, and a time to cast away;
>   a time to rend, and a time to sew;
>   a time to keep silence, and a time to speak;
>   a time to love, and a time to hate;
>   a time for war, and a time for peace.

(Ecclesiastes 3:1–8)

Selection 7

And God created man and woman in God's own image, male and female, God created them. Then God blessed them and said to them, "Be fertile and increase, fill the earth and master it". . . . And God saw what God created and found it very good.

(Genesis 1:27–28; 1:31)

Selection 8

Two are better than one,
Because they have a good reward for their labor.
For if they fall, one will lift up the other.

But woe to those who are alone when they fall,
For they have no one to help them up.

Again, if two lie down together, they will keep warm;
But how can one be warm alone?

(Ecclesiastes 4:9–12, adapted)

New Testament Passages

Selection 1

If I have all the eloquence of men and women or of angels, but speak without love, I am simply a gong booming or a cymbal clashing.

If I have the gift of prophecy, understanding all mysteries and knowing everything, and if I have all faith so as to move mountains, but am without love, I am nothing.

If I give away all I possess, and if I deliver my body to be burned, but am without love, I gain nothing.

Love is always patient and kind; it is never jealous or selfish, it does not take offense and is not resentful.

Love takes no pleasure in other people's sins, but delights in the truth. It is always ready to excuse, to trust, and to endure whatever comes. Love does not end.

There are in the end three things that last: Faith, Hope, and Love; and the greatest of these is Love.

(1 Corinthians 13:1–8a, 13:13)

Selection 2

Let love be genuine; hate what is evil, hold fast to what is
    good;
Love one another with affection. . . .
Rejoice in your hope, be patient in tribulation, be constant
    in prayer.

(Romans 12:9–13)

Selection 3

> Our God in heaven,
> Hallowed be your name,
> Your kingdom come,
> Your will be done,
> On earth as in heaven.
> Give us today our daily bread.
> And forgive us our trespasses,
> As we forgive those
> Who trespass against us,
> And lead us not into temptation,
> But deliver us from evil. Amen.

(The Lord's Prayer, Matthew 6:9–13)

Selection 4

In the beginning God made man and woman, male and female, and said, "For this reason a man shall leave his father and mother and be joined to his wife, and the two shall become one flesh." So they are no longer two, but one flesh. What therefore God has joined together, let no one put asunder.

(Matthew 19:4–6, adapted)

Modern Poetry and Prose

Selection 1

Let me not to the marriage of true minds
Admit impediments. Love is not love
Which alters when it alteration finds.
Or bends with the remover to remove.
O, no! It is an ever fixed mark,
That looks on tempests and is never shaken.
It is the star to every wandering bark
Whose worth's unknown, although his height be taken.
Love's not time's fool, though rosy lips and cheeks
Within his bending sickle's compass come;
Love alters not with his brief hours and weeks,
But bears it out even to the edge of doom.

("Sonnet CXVI," by William Shakespeare)

Selection 2

Love comes quietly
Finally, drops
About me, on me,
In the old ways.

What did I know
Thinking myself
Able to go
Alone all the way.

("Love Comes Quietly," by Robert Creeley)[1]

Selection 3

> Comerado, I give you my hand!
> I give you my love more precious than money,
> I give you myself before preaching or law;
> Will you give me yourself? Will you come travel with me?
> Shall we stick by each other as long as we live?
> (Excerpt from "Song of the Open Road," by Walt Whitman)

Selection 4

> Two such as you . . .
> Cannot be parted nor be swept away
> From one another once you are agreed
> That life is only life forevermore
> Together wing to wing and oar to oar.
> (Excerpt from "The Master Speed," by Robert Frost)[2]

Selection 5

> If thou must love me, let it be for nought
> Except for love's sake only. Do not say,
> "I love her for her smile—her look—her way
> Of speaking gently—for a trick or thought
> That falls in well with mine . . ."
> For these things in themselves, Beloved, may
> Be changed, or change for thee—and love, so wrought,
> May be unwrought so . . .
> ("Sonnet XIV," by Elizabeth Barrett Browning)

Selection 6

> The minute I heard my first love story
> I started looking for you, not knowing
> how blind I was.
>
> Lovers don't finally meet somewhere.
> They're in each other all along.
> (Excerpt from *Selections from the Mystical Poems of Rumi*,
> translated by Arberry)

Selection 7

But when two people are as one
in their innermost hearts,
They shatter even the strength
of iron or of bronze.
And when two people understand each other
in their innermost hearts,
Their words are sweet and strong
like the fragrance of orchids.

(Excerpt from the *I Ching*)

Selection 8

Now it is completed
The marriage ceremony,
Just like the moon descending
In its dazzling radiance.
The couple is given the happiness
Of those who watch
Which showers down upon them like gold.
This is the symbol,
The marriage ceremony,
With the blessings of all the guests,
That this marriage may be free from all misfortune
And bear eternal happiness forever.

(Javanese poem)

Selection 9

Now you will feel no rain,
for each of you will be shelter for the other.
Now you will feel no cold,
for each of you will be warmth to the other,
Now there is no more loneliness,
for each of you will be companion to the other.
Now you are two persons,
but there is only one life before you.
Go now to your dwelling to enter into
the days of your togetherness.

And may your days be good,
    and long upon the earth.

                            (Apache marriage poem)

Selection 10

somewhere i have never travelled,gladly beyond
any experience,your eyes have their silence:
in your most frail gesture are things which enclose me,
or which i cannot touch because they are too near

your slightest look easily will enclose me
though i have closed myself as fingers,
you open always petal by petal myself as Spring opens
(touching skilfully,mysteriously)her first rose

or if your wish be to close me,i and
my life will shut very beautifully,suddenly,
as when the heart of this flower imagines
the snow carefully everywhere descending;

nothing which we are to perceive in this world equals
the power of your intense fragility:whose texture
compels me with the colour of its countries,
rendering death and forever with each breathing

(i do not know what it is about you that closes
and opens;only something in me understands
the voice of your eyes is deeper than all roses)
nobody,not even the rain,has such small hands

                        ("LVII," by E. E. Cummings)

Selection 11

You are my husband/wife
My feet shall run because of you.
My feet dance because of you.
My heart shall beat because of you.
My eyes see because of you.

My mind, think because of you.
And I shall love because of you.

(Eskimo love song)

Selection 12

How do I love thee? Let me count the ways.
I love thee to the depth and breadth and height
My soul can reach, when feeling out of sight
For the ends of Being and ideal Grace.
I love thee to the level of everyday's
Most quiet need, by sun and candle light.
I love thee freely, as men strive for Right;
I love thee purely, as they turn from Praise.
I love thee with the passion put to use
In my old griefs, and with my childhood's faith.
I love thee with a love I seemed to lose
With my lost saints, I love thee with the breath,
Smiles, tears, of all my life! and, if God choose,
I shall but love thee better after death.

("Sonnet XLIII," by Elizabeth Barrett Browning)

Selection 13

Grow old with me!
The rest is yet to be,
The last of life, for which the first was made:
Our times are in his hand
Who saith, "A whole I planned,
Youth shows but half; trust God: see all, nor be afraid!"

(Excerpt from "Rabbi Ben Ezra," by Robert Browning)

Selection 14

I do not offer the old smooth prizes,
But offer rough new prizes,
These are the days that must happen to you:
You shall not heap up what is called riches,
You shall scatter with lavish hand all that you earn or
    achieve.

However sweet the laid-up stores,
However convenient the dwellings,
You shall not remain there.
However sheltered the port,
And however calm the waters,
You shall not anchor there.
However welcome the hospitality that welcomes you
You are permitted to receive it but a little while
Afoot and light-hearted, take the open road,
Healthy, free, the world before you,
The long brown path before you, leading wherever you choose.
Say only to one another:
Camerado, I give you my hand!
I give you my love, more precious than money,
I give you myself before preaching or law:
Will you give me yourself?
Will you come travel with me?
Shall we stick by each other as long as we live?
  (Excerpt from "Song of the Open Road," by Walt Whitman)

Selection 15

I do not love you as if you were salt-rose, or topaz,
or the arrow of carnations the fire shoots off.
I love you as certain dark things are to be loved,
in secret, between the shadow and the soul.

I love you as the plant that never blooms
but carries in itself the light of hidden flowers;
thanks to your love a certain solid fragrance,
risen from the earth, lives darkly in my body.

I love you without knowing how, or when, or from where.
I love you straightforwardly, without complexities or pride;
so I love you because I know no other way

than this: where *I* does not exist, nor *you*,
so close that your hand on my chest is my hand,

so close that your eyes close as I fall asleep.

> (Sonnet XVII from *100 Love Sonnets:*
> *Cien sonetos de amor*, by Pablo Neruda)[3]

Selection 16

Man and woman are like the earth, that brings forth flowers
  in summer, but underneath is rock,
Older than flowers, older than ferns, older than foraminiferae,
  older than plasm altogether is the soul underneath.

And when, throughout all the wild chaos of love
  slowly a gem forms, in the ancient, once-more-molten
  rocks of two human hearts, two ancient rocks, a man's
  heart and a woman's, that is the crystal of peace, the slow
  hard jewel of trust, the sapphire of fidelity.
The gem of mutual peace emerging from the wild chaos of love.

> (Excerpt from "Fidelity," by D. H. Lawrence)

Selection 17

A man from a town of Negua, on the coast of Colombia, could climb into the sky. On his return, he described his trip. He told how he had contemplated human life from on high. He said we are a sea of tiny flames. Each person shines with his or her own light. No two flames are alike. There are big flames and little flames, flames of every color. Some people's flames are so still they don't even flicker in the wind while others have wild flames that fill the air with sparks. Some foolish flames neither burn nor shed light, but blaze with life so fiercely that you can't look at them without blinking and if you approach, you shine in fire.

("The World," by Eduardo Galeano, translated by Cedric Belfrage)[4]

Selection 18

Remember in your commitment to share equally in the responsibilities and labors, as well as the good fortunes and joys of your life together. Each experience will come in its season, and you must stand by each other through them all.

Nurture strength of spirit to shield you in sudden misfortune, but do not distress yourself with imaginings. Many fears are born of fatigue and loneliness. Beyond a wholesome discipline be gentle with yourself.

Enjoy your achievements as well as your plans. Keep interested in your own career, however humble: it is a real possession in the changing fortunes of time.

Therefore be at peace with God, whatever you conceive that to be. For with all its sham, drudgery and broken dreams, it is still a beautiful world. Strive to be happy.

(Excerpt from "Desiderata," by Max Ehrmann)[5]

Selection 19

Let there be spaces in your togetherness
And let the winds of heaven dance between you.
Love one another, but make not a bond of love:
Let it rather be a moving sea between the shores of your
    souls.

Sing and dance together and be joyous,
But let each one of you be alone,
Even as the strings of a lute are alone,
Though they quiver with the same music.
Give your hearts, but not into each other's keeping.
For only the hand of Life can contain your hearts.
And stand together yet not too near together:
For the pillars of the temple stand apart,
And the oak tree and the cypress grow not in each other's
    shadow.

(Excerpt from *The Prophet*, by Kahlil Gibran)[6]

Selection 20

Experience has taught you that all your moments will not be filled with joy. Events beyond your control will test your strength. Different values, desires, and pressures will try your patience and compassion. Yet, if you remain open and honest with each other, then even the most difficult trial will not break the bond between you. With love and trust as foundations of your relationship, the storms can bring you closer together.

(Devon A. Lerner)

Selection 21

If each of you experience and share of yourself from the center of your existence, that is true communication . . . the basis for a love that is deep and alive. This kind of love is a constant challenge; it is not a resting place, but a moving, growing, working together. Two people are one with each other by being one with themselves.

(Excerpt from *The Art of Loving*, by Eric Fromm)

Selection 22

And let there be no purpose in friendship save the deepening of the spirit. . . . For it is for your friend to fill your need, but not your emptiness. And in the sweetness of friendship let there be laughter, and sharing of pleasures. For in the dew of little things, the heart finds its morning and is refreshed.

(Excerpt from *The Prophet*, by Kahlil Gibran)[7]

Selection 23

For one human being to love another: that is perhaps the hardest of all tasks, the ultimate test and proof, the work for which all other work is but preparation. . . . Love . . . is a high inducement to the individual to ripen, to become something in himself . . . (a) world to himself for another's sake . . . (Human love) consists in this, that two solitudes protect and touch and greet each other.

(Excerpt from *Letters to a Young Poet*, by Rainer Maria Rilke, translated by M. D. Herter Norton)[8]

Selection 24

What greater thing is there for two human souls than to feel that they are joined . . . to strengthen each other . . . (and) to be one with each other in silent unspeakable memories.

(George Eliot)

Selection 25

(Marriage is not a matter) . . . of creating a quick community of spirit by tearing down and destroying all boundaries, but rather a good marriage is that in which each appoints the other guardian of his solitude . . . once the realization is accepted that even between the closest human beings infinite distances continue to exist, a wonderful living side by side can grow, if they succeed in loving the distance between them . . . (no less than one another).

(Excerpt from *Letters to a Young Poet*, by Rainer Maria Rilke, translated by M. D. Herter Norton)[9]

Selection 26
Love is the life of the soul. It is the harmony of the universe.

(William Channing)

Selection 27
A good relationship has a pattern like a dance and is built on some of the same rules. The partners do not need to hold on tightly, because they move confidently in the same pattern, intricate but gay and swift and free, like a country dance of Mozart's. To touch heavily would be to arrest the pattern and freeze the movement, to check the endlessly changing beauty of its unfolding. There is no place here for the possessive clutch, the clinging arm, the heavy hand; only the barest touch in passing. Now arm in arm, now face to face, now back to back—it does not matter which. Because they know they are partners moving to the same rhythm, creating a pattern together, and being invisibly nourished by it.

(Excerpt from *Gift from the Sea*, by Anne Morrow Lindbergh)

Selection 28
Nothing happens without a cause. The union of this man and woman has not come about accidentally but is the foreordained result of many past lives. This tie can therefore not be broken or dissolved.

(Buddhist marriage homily)

Selection 29
I give you the life I have let live for love of you . . .

(Excerpt from "The Country Marriage," by Wendell Berry)

Selection 30
The world rolls; the circumstances vary every hour. . . . (The lovers') once flaming regard is sobered . . . and losing in violence what it gains in extent, it becomes a thorough good understanding. At last (the lovers)

discover that all which at first drew them together, those once sacred features, that magical play of charms, had a prospective end, like the scaffolding by which the house was built, and the purification of the intellect and the heart, from year to year, is the real marriage. . . .

(Ralph Waldo Emerson)

Selection 31

When you love someone, you do not love them all the time, in exactly the same way, from moment to moment. It is an impossibility, it is even a lie to pretend to. And yet this is exactly what most of us demand. We have so little faith in the ebb and flow of life, of love, of relationships. We leap at the flow of the tide and resist in terror its ebb. We are afraid it will never return. We insist on permanency, on duration, on continuity; when the only continuity possible in life, as in love, is in growth, in fluidity, in freedom, in the sense that the dancers are free, barely touching as they pass, but partners in the same pattern.

The only real security is not in owning or possessing, not in demanding or expecting, not in hoping even. Security in a relationship lies neither in looking back to what it was in nostalgia, nor forward to what it might be in dread or anticipation, but living in the present relationship and accepting it as it is now. For relationships, too, must be like islands. One must accept them for what they are here and now, within their limits. Islands, surrounded and interrupted by the sea, are continually visited and abandoned by the tides. One must accept the security of the winged life, of the ebb an flow, of intermittency.

(Anne Morrow Lindbergh)

Selection 32

Suddenly she said to him with extraordinary beauty: "I engage myself to you forever."

The beauty was in everything, and he could have separated nothing, couldn't have thought of her face as distinct from the whole joy. Yet her face had a new light. "And I pledge you every spark of my faith, I give you every drop of my life." That was all, for the moment, but it was enough, and it was almost as quiet as if it were nothing. They were in the open air, in an alley of the Gardens; the great space, which seemed to arch just then higher and spread wider for them, threw them, threw them back into deep concentration. There, before their time together was spent, they extorted from concentration every advance it could make them. They exchanged vows and tokens, sealed their rich compact, solemnized, so far as breathed words and lighted eyes and clasped hands could do it, their agreement to belong only, and to belong tremendously, to each other.

(Excerpt from *The Wings of the Dove*, by Henry James)

Selection 33
[Then the little prince saw a garden of roses.] "You are not at all like my rose," he said. "As yet you are nothing. No one has tamed you, and you have tamed no one. You are like my fox when I first knew him. He was only a fox like a hundred thousand other foxes. But I have made him my friend, and now he is unique in all the world. . . .

"You are beautiful, but you are empty," he went on. "One could not die for you. To be sure, an ordinary passerby would think that my rose looked just like you—the rose that belongs to me. But in herself alone she is more important than all the hundreds of other roses: because it is she that I have watered . . . because it is she that I have sheltered . . . because it is she that I have listened to, when she grumbled, or boasted, or even sometimes when she said nothing. Because she is *my* rose."

And he went back to meet the fox.

"Goodbye," he said.

"Goodbye," said the fox. "And now here is my secret, a very simple secret: it is only with the heart that one can see rightly; what is essential is invisible to the eye. . . .

"It is the time you have wasted for your rose that makes your rose so important. . . .

"You become responsible, forever, for what you have tamed. You are responsible for your rose."

(Excerpt from *The Little Prince*, by Antoine de Saint-Exupery, translation by Katherine Woods)[10]

· APPENDIX I ·

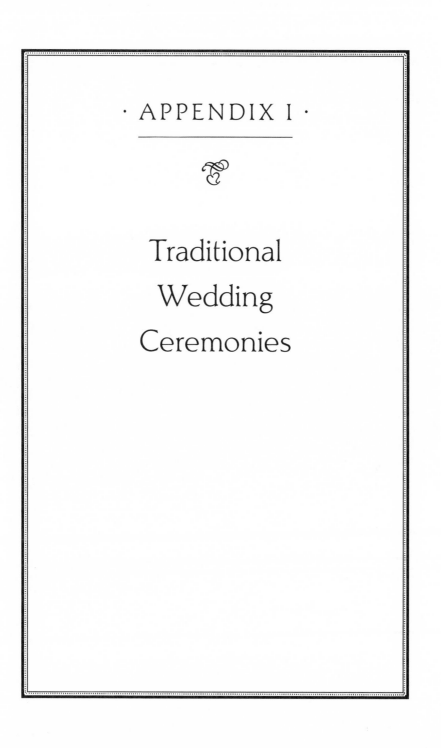

Traditional
Wedding
Ceremonies

A Reform Jewish Wedding

❦

Officiated by a Rabbi
(Time: approximately 20 minutes)

1. Opening Blessing
2. Explanation of the Huppah
3. Shehecheyanu, a Special Prayer Recited at Joyous Occasions
4. Remarks by the Rabbi
5. Blessing over the Wine, Including a Blessing of the Couple under the Huppah
6. Exchange of Vows
7. Exchange of Rings, Using the Traditional Formula called the Haray Aht
8. Seven Wedding Blessings in Hebrew and English
9. Pronouncement
10. Silent Prayer
11. Benediction
12. Breaking of the Glass

Opening Blessing

בְּרוּכִים הַבָּאִים בְּשֵׁם יְיָ.

Blessed are you who come here in the name of God.

עִבְדוּ אֶת יְיָ בְּשִׂמְחָה. בֹּאוּ לְפָנָיו בִּרְנָנָה.

Serve God with joy, come into God's presence with song.

מִי אַדִּיר עַל הַכֹּל. מִי בָרוּךְ עַל הַכֹּל. מִי גָדוֹל עַל הַכֹּל.
הוּא יְבָרֵךְ אֶת-הֶחָתָן וְאֶת-הַכַּלָּה.

O most awesome, glorious and blessed God, grant Your blessings to the bride and groom.

Explanation of the Huppah

Surrounded by loved ones whose joy and prayers are with you, you
stand at this huppah, symbol of the Jewish home. May your home be
a shelter against the storms, a haven of peace, a stronghold of faith
and love.[1]

Shehecheyanu, a Special Prayer
Recited at Joyous Occasions

בָּרוּךְ אַתָּה יְיָ אֱלֹהֵינוּ מֶלֶךְ הָעוֹלָם שֶׁהֶחֱיָנוּ וְקִיְּמָנוּ וְהִגִּיעָנוּ
לַזְּמַן הַזֶּה.

Blessed are you, O God, for giving life, sustaining us and
bringing us to this joyous time.

Remarks by the Rabbi

*[The rabbi typically comments on the nature of love and marriage,
adding a few personal notes, when possible.]*

Blessing over the Wine

This cup of wine is symbolic of the cup of life. As you share the one cup of
wine, you undertake to share all that the future may bring. All the sweet-

ness life's cup may hold for you should be sweeter because you drink it together; whatever drops of bitterness it may contain should be less bitter because your share them.

As I recite the blessing over the wine, we pray that God will bestow fullness of joy upon you.[2]

בָּרוּךְ אַתָּה יְיָ אֱלֹהֵינוּ מֶלֶךְ הָעוֹלָם בּוֹרֵא פְּרִי הַגָּפֶן.

We praise you, (O Lord) our God, Ruler of the universe, Creator of the fruit of the vine.

[Bride and groom take a sip of wine.]

Exchange of Vows

[These "vows" are a late addition to the Reform Jewish wedding liturgy. Originally, the words exchanged with the rings were considered to be the vows as well.]

Do you, (groom), take (bride) to be your wife, promising to cherish and protect her, whether in good fortune or in adversity, and to seek together with her a life hallowed by the faith of Israel?

And do you, (bride), take (groom) to be your husband, promising to cherish and protect him whether in good fortune or in adversity, and to seek together with him a life hallowed by the faith of Israel?

Ring Ceremony

In keeping with the declaration you have made, you give and receive these rings. They are tokens of your union, a symbol of enduring loyalty. May they ever remind you that your lives are bound together by devotion and faithfulness.

As you, (groom/bride), place this ring on (bride/groom)'s finger, repeat after me:

הֲרֵי אַתְּ מְקוּדֶּשֶׁת (אַתָּה מְקֻדָּשׁ) לִי בְּטַבַּעַת זוֹ כְּדַת מֹשֶׁה וְיִשְׂרָאֵל.

With this ring, be consecrated to me as my wife/husband according to the heritage of Moses and Israel.

[This phrase, "With this ring . . . ," known as the Haray Aht, is considered by many Jews to be the essential part of a Jewish wedding ceremony.]

בָּרוּךְ אַתָּה יְיָ מְקַדֵּשׁ עַמּוֹ עַל-יְדֵי חֻפָּה וְקִדּוּשִׁין.

We praise You, Our God, who hallows our people Israel through the sacred rite at the huppah.³

Seven Wedding Blessings in Hebrew and English

As I recite the seven wedding blessings, we all pray that God will grant you fulfillment and joy.

בָּרוּךְ אַתָּה יְיָ אֱלֹהֵינוּ מֶלֶךְ הָעוֹלָם בּוֹרֵא פְּרִי הַגָּפֶן.

Blessed are you, (Adonai or Lord) our God, Ruler of the universe, Creator of the fruit of the vine.

בָּרוּךְ אַתָּה יְיָ אֱלֹהֵינוּ מֶלֶךְ הָעוֹלָם שֶׁהַכֹּל בָּרָא לִכְבוֹדוֹ.

We praise you, (O Lord) our God, Ruler of the universe, Creator of all things for Your glory.

בָּרוּךְ אַתָּה יְיָ אֱלֹהֵינוּ מֶלֶךְ הָעוֹלָם יוֹצֵר הָאָדָם.

We praise you, (O Lord) our God, Ruler of the universe, Creator of man and woman.

בָּרוּךְ אַתָּה יְיָ אֱלֹהֵינוּ מֶלֶךְ הָעוֹלָם, אֲשֶׁר יָצַר אֶת־הָאָדָם
בְּצַלְמוֹ, בְּצֶלֶם דְּמוּת תַּבְנִיתוֹ, וְהִתְקִין לוֹ מִמֶּנּוּ בִּנְיַן עֲדֵי עַד
בָּרוּךְ אַתָּה יְיָ יוֹצֵר הָאָדָם.

We praise you, (O Lord) our God, Ruler of the universe, who
creates us to share with You in life's everlasting renewal.

שׂוֹשׂ תָּשִׂישׂ וְתָגֵל צִיּוֹן בְּקִבּוּץ בָּנֶיהָ לְתוֹכָהּ בְּשִׂמְחָה בָּרוּךְ
אַתָּה יְיָ מְשַׂמֵּחַ צִיּוֹן בְּבָנֶיהָ.

We praise you, (O Lord) our God, Ruler of the universe, who
causes Zion to rejoice in her children's happy return.

שַׂמֵּחַ תְּשַׂמַּח רֵעִים הָאֲהוּבִים כְּשַׂמֵּחֲךָ יְצִירְךָ בְּגַן עֵדֶן מִקֶּדֶם.
בָּרוּךְ אַתָּה יְיָ מְשַׂמֵּחַ חָתָן וְכַלָּה.

We praise you, (O Lord) our God, Ruler of the universe,
who causes bride and groom to rejoice. May these loving
companions rejoice as have Your creatures since the days of
creation.

בָּרוּךְ אַתָּה יְיָ אֱלֹהֵינוּ מֶלֶךְ הָעוֹלָם, אֲשֶׁר בָּרָא שָׂשׂוֹן
וְשִׂמְחָה, חָתָן וְכַלָּה, גִּילָה רִנָּה דִּיצָה וְחֶדְוָה, אַהֲבָה
וְאַחֲוָה, שָׁלוֹם וְרֵעוּת. מְהֵרָה יְיָ אֱלֹהֵינוּ יִשָּׁמַע בְּעָרֵי
יְהוּדָה וּבְחוּצוֹת יְרוּשָׁלַיִם, קוֹל שָׂשׂוֹן וְקוֹל שִׂמְחָה, קוֹל
חָתָן וְקוֹל כַּלָּה, קוֹל מִצְהֲלוֹת חֲתָנִים מֵחֻפָּתָם וּנְעָרִים
מִמִּשְׁתֵּה נְגִינָתָם. בָּרוּךְ אַתָּה יְיָ מְשַׂמֵּחַ חָתָן עִם־הַכַּלָּה.

We praise you, (O Lord) our God, Ruler of the universe, Creator of joy and gladness, bride and groom, love and kinship,
peace and friendship. O God, may there always be heard in
the cities of Israel and in the streets of Jerusalem: the sounds
of joy and of happiness, the voice of the groom and the voice
of the bride, the shouts of young people celebrating, and the
songs of children at play. We praise you, our God, who causes
bride and groom to rejoice together.[4]

בָּרוּךְ אַתָּה יְיָ אֱלֹהֵינוּ מֶלֶךְ הָעוֹלָם בּוֹרֵא פְּרִי הַגָּפֶן.

Blessed are you, Our God, Creator of the fruit of the vine.

[Bride and groom take a sip of wine.]

As you have shared this cup of wine, so may you, under God's guidance, share contentment, peace and fulfillment from the cup of life. May you find life's joys heightened, its bitterness sweetened, and each of its moments hallowed by true companionship and love.[5]

Pronouncement

In the presence of these witnesses and in keeping with our tradition, you have spoken the words and performed the rites that unite your lives. (Groom and bride), you are now husband and wife in the sight of God, the Jewish community, and all people.[6]

Silent Prayer

I now ask you and all your friends and family to take a moment to silently pray that your home will be blessed and that you will achieve your highest hopes.

Benediction in Hebrew and English

[This blessing, known as the "Priestly Blessing," is common to both Jewish and Christian liturgies.]

יְבָרֶכְךָ יְיָ וְיִשְׁמְרֶךָ.

May God bless you and keep you.

יָאֵר יְיָ פָּנָיו אֵלֶיךָ וִיחֻנֶּךָ.

May God's countenance shine upon you and be gracious to you.

יִשָּׂא יְיָ פָּנָיו אֵלֶיךָ וְיָשֵׂם לְךָ שָׁלוֹם.

May God look upon you with favor and grant you peace.

Breaking of the Glass

*[There are many explanations to the breaking of the glass.
See "Breaking of the Glass," in Part III for examples.]*

A Roman Catholic Wedding

☙

Outside Mass
The Rite of Marriage Between a Catholic
and an Unbaptized Person

Gathering and Entrance Rites
1. Rite of Welcome

Liturgy of the Word
2. Hebrew Scripture Reading
3. Responsorial Psalm
4. New Testament Reading(s)
5. Homily

Marriage Rite
6. Introduction
7. Consent
8. Exchange of Rings
9. General Intercessions
10. Nuptial Blessing

Concluding Rites
11. The Lord's Prayer
12. Concluding Blessing

Gathering and Entrance Rites

THE RITE OF WELCOME

[At the appointed time, the priest proceeds with the ministers to the door of the church or to another appropriate place and greets the bride and the bridegroom, or the celebration of marriage begins immediately with the liturgy of the word.]

Liturgy of the Word

HEBREW SCRIPTURE

[The liturgy of the word takes place in the usual manner. There may be three readings, or, if circumstances make it more desirable, there may be a single reading drawn from the marriage ritual. The following passages are provided by way of example:]

God said: "Let us make man beings in our image, after our likeness. Let them have dominion over the fish of the sea, the birds of the air, and the cattle, and over all the wild animals and all the creatures that crawl on the ground."

God created man in his image: in the divine image God created him; male and female he created them.

God blessed them, saying: "Be fertile and multiply; fill the earth and subdue it. Have dominion over the fish of the sea, the birds of the air, and all the living things that move on the earth." God looked at everything he had made, and he found it very good.

(Genesis 1:26–28, 31)

Reader:
The word of the Lord.

All:
Thanks be to God.

RESPONSORIAL PSALM

[The following is only one of several possible responsorial selections.]

Response:
The Lord is compassionate to all his creatures.

Priest:
The Lord is gracious and merciful,
    slow to anger and of great kindness.
The Lord is good to all
    and compassionate toward all his works.

Response:
The Lord is compassionate to all his creatures.

Priest:
Let all your works give you thanks, O Lord,
    and let your faithful ones bless you.
The eyes of all look hopefully to you,
    and you give them their food in due season.

Response:
The Lord is compassionate to all his creatures.

Priest:
The Lord is just in all his ways
    and holy in all his works.
The Lord is near to all who call upon him,
    to all who call upon him in truth.

Response:
The Lord is compassionate to all his creatures.

(Psalms 145:8–9, 10, 15, 17–18)

NEW TESTAMENT READING

Set your hearts on the greater gifts. I will show you the way which surpasses all the others. If I speak with human tongues and angelic as well, but do not have love, I am a noisy gong, a clanging cymbal. If I have the gift of prophecy and, with full knowledge, comprehend all mysteries; if I have faith great enough to move mountains, but have not love, I am nothing. If I give everything to feed the poor and hand over my body to be burned, but have not love, I gain nothing.

Love is patient; love is kind. Love is not jealous, it does not put on airs, it is not snobbish. Love is never rude, it is not self-seeking, it is not prone to anger; neither does it brood over injuries. Love does not rejoice in what is wrong but rejoices with the truth. There is no limit to love's forbearance, to its trust, its hope, its power to endure.

Love never fails.

(1 Corinthians 12:31–13:8)

Reader:
The Word of the Lord.

All:
Thanks be to God.

HOMILY

[The priest uses the biblical readings as a springboard for his comments to the couple on the sacramental nature of a Christian marriage. He may also add some personal remarks, especially when he knows the couple well.]

Marriage Rite

INTRODUCTION

Priest:
My dear friends, you have come together in this church so that the Lord may seal and strengthen your love in the presence of the Church's minister and this community. In this way, you will be strengthened to keep mutual and lasting faith with each other and to carry out the other duties of marriage. And so, in the presence of this Church, I ask you to state your intentions.

(Bride) and (groom), have you come here freely and without reservation to give yourselves to each other in marriage?

Bride and Groom:
We have.

Priest:
Will you love and honor each other as husband and wife for the rest of your lives?

Bride and Groom:
We will.

CONSENT

Priest:
Since it is your intention to enter into marriage, join your right hands, and declare your consent before god and the Church.

[The bride and groom join right hands.]

Groom, then bride:
I, (groom/bride), take you, (bride/groom), to be my wife/husband. I promise to be true to you in good times and in bad, in sickness and in health. I will love you and honor you all the days of my life.

Priest:
You have declared your consent before the Church. May the Lord in his goodness strengthen your consent and fill you both with his blessings. What God has joined, no one must divide.

All:
Amen.

EXCHANGE OF RINGS

Priest:
May the Lord bless these rings which we give to each other as the sign of your love and fidelity.

All:
Amen.

[The bride and groom place the ring on each other's finger.]

(Bride/groom), take this ring as a sign of my love and fidelity. In the name of the Father, and of the Son, and of the Holy Spirit.

GENERAL INTERCESSIONS

[These are prayers directed to the larger needs of the world, the church and our communities. They are often written by the priest, members of the parish, or by the wedding couple themselves. These prayers might include a prayer for deceased and/or sick relatives; for parents, godparents, and other important people in your lives. Prayers are also added for societal concerns and issues, such as the poor, the homeless, and the unemployed, and for peace among nations. Usually there are five or six intentions. Each is followed by the reader saying: Let us pray to the Lord. The assembly responds: Lord, hear our prayer. The following is one example of general intercessions.]

For the outcasts and the downtrodden of our city and our nation, that they may find refuge and compassion in our churches and families, we pray to the Lord.

All respond:
Lord, hear our prayer.

For family members who have gone before us marked with the sign of faith, especially (deceased relatives), that our prayer today may be joined with theirs, we pray to the Lord.

All respond:
Lord, hear our prayer.

For (bride) and (groom), that the Lord bless them with many happy years together, we pray to the Lord.

All respond:
Lord, hear our prayer.

NUPTIAL BLESSING

My dear friends, let us ask God for his continued blessing upon this bride-groom and bride.

Holy Father, creator of the universe, maker of man and woman in your likeness, source of blessing for married life, we humbly pray to you for this bride who today is united with her husband in the bond of marriage.

May your fullest blessing come upon her and her husband so that they may together rejoice in your gift of married love.

Lord, may they be noted for their good lives (and be parents filled with virtue).

Lord, may they both praise you when they are happy, and turn to you in their sorrows. May they be glad that you help them in their work and know that you are with them in their need. May they reach old age in the company of their friends, and come at last to the kingdom of heaven. We ask this through Christ our Lord. Amen.

Concluding Rites

THE LORD'S PRAYER

Priest:
Our Father who art in heaven, hallowed be thy Name,
Thy kingdom come, thy will be done, on earth as it is in
heaven.

Give us this day our daily bread.
And forgive us our trespasses, as we forgive those who
trespass against us.

And lead us not into temptation
But deliver us from evil. Amen.

CONCLUDING PRAYER FOR THE MARRIED COUPLE

Priest:
May almighty God, with his Word of blessing, unite your
hearts in the never-ending bond of pure love.

All respond:
Amen.

Priest:
May your children bring you happiness, and may your generous love for them be returned to you, many times over.

All respond:
Amen.

Priest:
May the peace of Christ live always in your hearts and in your
home. May you have true friends to stand by you, both in
joy and in sorrow. May you be ready and willing to help and

comfort all who come to you in need. And may the blessings promised to the compassionate be yours in abundance.

All respond:
Amen.

Priest:

May you find happiness and satisfaction in your work. May daily problems never cause you undue anxiety, nor the desire for earthly possessions dominate your lives. But may your hearts' first desire be always the good things waiting for you in the life of heaven.

All respond:
Amen.

Priest:

May the Lord bless you with many happy years together, so that you may enjoy the rewards of a good life. And after you have served him loyally in his kingdom on earth, may he welcome you to his eternal kingdom in heaven.

All respond:
Amen.

Priest:

And may almighty God bless you all, the Father, and the Son, and the Holy Spirit.

All respond:
Amen.

[The priest ends the ceremony with the following statement.]

Go in the peace of Christ.[1]

An Episcopal Wedding

1. Opening Remarks
2. Declaration of Consent
3. Affirmation of the Congregation
4. Ministry of the Word
    Hebrew Scripture Reading
    Psalm or Hymn
    New Testament Reading
5. Homily
6. Exchange of Vows
7. Exchange of Rings
8. Pronouncement
9. The Lord's Prayer
10. Blessing of the Couple
11. Blessing of the Marriage

Opening Remarks

[The priest usually begins with an informal greeting of the guests.]

Priest:
Dearly Beloved: We have come together in the presence of God to witness and bless the joining together of this man and woman in holy matrimony. The bond and covenant of marriage was established by God in Creation, and our Lord Jesus Christ adorned this manner of life by His

presence and first miracle at a wedding in Cana of Galilee. It signifies to us the mystery of the union between Christ and His Church, and Holy Scripture commends it to be honored among all people.

The union of husband and wife in heart, body, and mind is intended by God for their mutual joy; for the help and comfort given one another in prosperity and adversity; and, when it is God's will, for the procreation of children and their nurture in the knowledge and love of the Lord. Therefore, marriage is not to be entered into unadvisedly or lightly, but reverently, deliberately, and in accordance with the purposes for which it was instituted by God.

Into this union (bride) and (groom) now come to be joined. If any of you can show just cause why they may not lawfully be married, speak now; or else forever hold your peace.

[To the bride and groom:]

I require and charge you both, here in the presence of God, that if either of you knows any reason why you should not be united in marriage lawfully, and in accordance with God's Word, you do now confess it.

Declaration of Consent

[To the groom and then to the bride:]

Priest:
(Groom/bride), will you have this woman/man to be your wife/husband; to live together in the covenant of marriage? Will you love her/him, comfort her/him, honor and keep her/him, in sickness and in health; and forsaking all others, be faithful to her/him as long as you both shall live?

Groom/bride:
I will.

Affirmation of the Congregation

Priest:
Will all of you witnessing these promises do all in your power to uphold these two persons in their marriage?

Guests:
We will.

Ministry of the Word

Priest:
The Lord be with you.

Guests:
And also with you.

Priest:
Let us pray. O gracious and ever-living God, you have created us male and female in your image: Look mercifully upon this man and this woman who come to you seeking your blessing, and assist them with your grace, that with true fidelity and steadfast love they may honor and keep the promises and vows they make; through Jesus Christ our Savior, who lives and reigns with you in the unity of the Holy Spirit, one God, for ever and ever. Amen.

HEBREW SCRIPTURE READING

[There are many possible selections, the two most frequently used are Genesis 1:26–28 (Male and female God created them), and Genesis 2:4–9, 15–24 (A man cleaves to his wife and they become one flesh.)]

PSALM OR HYMN

[Music: A psalm, hymn, or anthem is sung.]

NEW TESTAMENT READING

[The most frequently used passage is 1 Corinthians 13:1–13
(Love is patient and kind.)]

Exchange of Vows

[The bride and groom face each other and join their right hands.]

Bride/groom:
In the Name of God, I, (bride/groom), take you, (groom/bride), to be my
husband/wife, to have and to hold from this day forward, for better for
worse, for richer for poorer, in sickness and in health, to love and to cherish, until we are parted by death. This is my solemn vow.

Exchange of Rings

Priest:
Bless, O Lord, this ring to be a sign of the vows by which this man and
this woman have bound themselves to each other, through Jesus Christ
our Lord. Amen.

[Groom/bride places the ring on the ring finger of his/her partner.]

Bride/groom:
(Groom/bride), I give you this ring as a symbol of my vow, and with all
that I am, and all that I have, I honor you, in the Name of the Father, and
of the Son, and of the Holy Spirit (or in the Name of God).

Pronouncement

[Priest joins the right hands of the bride and groom.]

Priest:
Now that (bride) and (groom) have given themselves to each other by
solemn vows, with the joining of hands and the giving and receiving of a
ring, I pronounce that they are husband and wife, in the name of the

Father, and of the Son, and of the Holy Spirit. Those whom God had joined together, let no one put asunder. Amen.

The Lord's Prayer

Our Father in heaven, hallowed be your name,
Your kingdom come, your will be done, on earth as in
heaven.

Give us today our daily bread.
Forgive us our sins, as we forgive those who sin against us.

Save us from the time of trial, and deliver us from evil.
For the kingdom, the power, and the glory are yours,
now and forever. Amen.

Blessing of the Couple

Let us pray. Eternal God, Creator and Preserver of all life, Author of salvation, and Giver of grace: Look with favor upon the world you have made, and for which your Son gave his life, and especially upon this man and this woman whom you made one flesh in holy matrimony. Amen.

Give them the wisdom and devotion in the ordering of their common life, that each may be to the other a strength in need, a counselor in perplexity, a comfort in sorrow, and a companion in joy. Amen.

Grant that their wills may be so knit together in your will, and their spirits in your Spirit, that they may grow in love and peace with you and one another all the days of their life. Amen.

Give them grace, when they hurt each other, to recognize and acknowledge their fault, and to seek each other's forgiveness and yours. Amen.

Make their life together be a sign of Christ's love to this sinful and broken world, that unity may overcome estrangement, forgiveness heal guilt, and joy conquer despair. Amen.

(Bestow on them, if it is your will, the gift and heritage of children, and the grace to bring them up to know you, to love you, and to serve you. Amen.)

Give them such fulfillment of their mutual affection that they may reach out in love and concern for others. Amen.

Grant that all married persons who have witnessed these vows may find their lives strengthened and their loyalties confirmed. Amen.

Grant that the bonds of our common humanity, by which all your children are united one to another, and the living to the dead, may be so transformed by your grace, that your will may be done on earth as it is in heaven; where, O Father, with your Son and the Holy Spirit, you live and reign in perfect unity, now and forever. Amen.

Blessing of the Marriage

[The people remain standing. The husband and wife kneel, and the priest says this or another prayer.]

Priest:

O God, you have so consecrated the covenant of marriage that in it is represented the spiritual unity between Christ and his Church; Send therefore your blessing upon these your servants, that they may so love, honor, and cherish each other in faithfulness and patience, in wisdom and true godliness, that their home may be a haven of blessing and peace; through Jesus Christ our Lord, who lives and reigns with you and the Holy Spirit, one God, now and forever. Amen.

God the Father, God the Son, God the Holy Spirit, bless, preserve, and keep you; the Lord mercifully with his favor look upon you, and fill you with all spiritual benediction and grace; that you may faithfully live together in this life, and in the age to come have life everlasting. Amen.

The peace of the Lord be always with you.

Guests:

And also with you.[1]

A Presbyterian Wedding

☞

1. Call to Worship
2. Opening Remarks
3. Opening Prayer for the Couple
4. Declaration of Intent or Consent
5. Affirmation of the Families (asking the families to support the couple in their marriage)
6. Affirmation of the Congregation (asking the congregation to support the couple in their marriage)
7. Scripture Readings
8. Sermon or Homily
9. Exchange of Vows
10. Exchange of Rings
11. Blessing of the Couple
12. The Lord's Prayer
13. Pronouncement
14. Charge to the Couple
15. Closing Blessing

Call to Worship

[Congregation rises.]

Minister:
This is the day that the Lord has made; let us rejoice and be glad in it.

Opening Remarks

*[The minister usually begins with an
informal greeting of the guests.]*

Minister:
We gather in the presence of God to give thanks for the gift of marriage, to witness the joining together of (bride) and (groom) to surround them with our prayers, and to ask God's blessing upon them, so that they may be strengthened for their life together and nurtured in their love for God.

God created us male and female, and gave us marriage so that husband and wife may help and comfort each other, living faithfully together in plenty and in want, in joy and in sorrow, in sickness and in health, throughout all their days.

God gave us marriage for the full expression of the love between a man and a woman. In marriage a woman and a man belong to each other, and with affection and tenderness freely give themselves to each other.

God gave us marriage for the well-being of human society, for the ordering of family life, and for the birth and nurture of children. God gave us marriage as a holy mystery in which a man and a woman are joined together, and become one, just as Christ is one with the church.

In marriage, husband and wife are called to a new way of life, created, ordered and blessed by God. This way of life must not be entered into carelessly, or from selfish motives, but responsibly, and prayerfully.

We rejoice that marriage is given by God, blessed by our Lord Jesus Christ, and sustained by the Holy Spirit. Therefore, let marriage be held in honor by all.

Opening Prayer for the Couple

Minister:
Let us pray:
Gracious God, you are always faithful in your love for us.

Look mercifully upon (bride) and (groom), who have come seeking your blessing. Let your Holy Spirit rest upon them so that with steadfast

love they may honor the promises they make this day, through Jesus
Christ our Savior.
Amen.

[Congregation is seated.]

Declaration of Intent or Consent

[Minister says to the bride and to the groom individually:]

Minister:
(Groom/bride), understanding that God has created, ordered, and
blessed the covenant of marriage, do you affirm your desire and intention
to enter this covenant?

Groom/bride:
I do.

[If both are baptized, the following may be used:]

Minister:
(Groom/bride), in your baptism you have been called to union with
Christ and the church. Do you intend to honor this calling through the
covenant of marriage?

Groom/bride:
I do.

Affirmation of the Families

Minister:
(Names of family members), do you give your blessing to (bride) and
(groom) and promise to do everything in your power to uphold them in
their marriage?

Family members:
We give our blessing and promise our loving support.

or

We do.

Affirmation of the Congregation

Minister:
Will all of you witnessing these vows do everything in your power to uphold (bride) and (groom) in their marriage?

Congregation:
We will.

[Music: a psalm or anthem.]

Scripture Readings

Minister:
God of mercy, your faithfulness to your covenant frees us to live together in the security of your powerful love. Amid all the changing words of our generation, speak your eternal Word that does not change. Then may we respond to your gracious promises by living in faith and obedience: through our Lord Jesus Christ.
    Amen.

[Scripture readings.]

Sermon or Homily

[Based on the Scripture readings and related to marriage. The minister may also add some personal remarks, especially if she/he knows the couple well.]

Exchange of Vows

[Congregation stands.]

Minister:
(Bride) and (groom), since it is your intention to marry, join your right hands, and with your promises bind yourselves to each other as husband and wife.

Groom/bride:
I, (groom), take you, (bride), to be my wife/husband; and I promise, before God and these witnesses, to be your loving and faithful husband/ wife; in plenty and in want; in joy and in sorrow; in sickness and in health; as long as we both shall live.

Exchange of Rings

Minister:
By your blessing, O God, may these rings be to (bride) and (groom) symbols of unending love and faithfulness, reminding them of the covenant they have made this day, through Jesus Christ our Lord.
Amen.

[The traditional Trinitarian formula should be omitted for both the bride and groom if one of the marriage partners is not a professing Christian.]

Groom/bride:
I give you this ring as a sign of our covenant, in the name of the Father, and of the Son, and of the Holy Spirit.

Bride/groom:
I receive this ring as a sign of our covenant, in the name of the Father, and of the Son, and of the Holy Spirit.

Blessing of the Couple

[The couple may kneel.]

Minister:

Eternal God, Creator and Preserver of all life, Author of salvation, and Giver of all grace: look with favor upon the world you have made and redeemed, and especially upon (bride) and (groom). Give them wisdom and devotion in their common life, that each may be to the other a strength in need, a counselor in perplexity, a comfort in sorrow, and a companion in joy.

Grant that their wills may be so knit together in your will, and their spirits in your Spirit, that they may grow in love and peace with you and each other all the days of their life.

Give them the grace, when they hurt each other, to recognize and confess their fault, and to seek each other's forgiveness and yours. Make their life together a sign of Christ's love to this sinful and broken world, that unity may overcome estrangement, forgiveness heal guilt, and joy conquer despair.

Give them such fulfillment of their mutual love that they may reach out in concern for others. Give to them, if it is your will, the gift of children, and the wisdom to bring them up to know you, to love you, and to serve you.

Grant that all who have witnessed these vows today may find their lives strengthened, and that all who are married may depart with their own promises renewed. Enrich with your grace all husbands, wives, parents, and children, that, loving and supporting one another, they may serve those in need and be a sign of your kingdom.

Grant that the bonds by which all your children are united to one another may be so transformed by your Spirit that your peace and justice may fill the earth, through Jesus Christ our Lord.

The Lord's Prayer

[All pray together.]

Congregation and minister:
Our Father in heaven, hallowed be your Name,
Your kingdom come, your will be done, on earth as in
heaven.

Give us today our daily bread.
Forgive us our sins, as we forgive those who sin against us.

Save us from the time of trial, and deliver us from evil.
For the kingdom, the power, and the glory are yours,
now and forever. Amen.

Pronouncement

Minister:
Before God and in the presence of this congregation, (bride) and (groom)
have made their solemn vows to each other. They have confirmed their
promises by the joining of hands and by the giving and receiving of rings.
Therefore, I proclaim that they are now husband and wife.

Blessed be the Father, and the Son and the Holy Spirit, now and
forever.

[The minister joins the couple's right hands.]

Those whom God has joined together, let no one separate.

Charge to the Couple

Minister:
Whatever you do, in work or deed,
do everything in the name of the Lord Jesus,
giving thanks to God through him.

Closing Blessing

Minister:
The Lord bless you and keep you.
The Lord be kind and gracious to you.
The Lord look upon you with favor and give you peace.[1]

· APPENDIX II ·

Ketubot

Orthodox Ketubah

꩜

The following is the text of a traditional Orthodox ketubah. It is, in essence, a prenuptial agreement that the groom makes with his bride. In case of divorce, the bride will receive all the material goods listed. Love is never mentioned.

Today, most Jewish couples are signing new ketubot that speak directly about their love and commitment.

On the _____ day of the week, the _____ day of the month _____ in the year five thousand seven hundred and _____ since the creation of the world according to the reckoning which we are accustomed to use here in the city of _____ in _____. _____ son of _____ of the family _____ said to this maiden _____ daughter of _____ of the family _____,

"Be my wife according to the law of Moses and Israel, and I will cherish, honor, support, and maintain you in accordance with the custom of Jewish husbands, who cherish, honor, support, and maintain their wives faithfully. And I here present you with the marriage gift of virgins, two hundred silver zuzim, which belongs to you, according to the law of Moses and Israel; and I will also give you your food, clothing, and necessities, and live with you as husband and wife according to the universal custom."

And _____, this maiden consented and became his wife. The trousseau that she brought to him from her father's house in silver, gold,

valuables, clothing, furniture, and bedclothes, all this _____,
the bridegroom accepted in the sum of one hundred silver pieces, and
_____, the bridegroom, consented to increase this amount from
his own property with the sum of one hundred silver pieces, making in all
two hundred silver pieces. And thus said _____, the bridegroom:

"The responsibility of this marriage contract, of this trousseau, and of
this additional sum, I take upon myself and my heirs after me, so that
they shall be paid from the best part of my property and possessions that I
have beneath the whole heaven, that which I now possess or may here-
after acquire. All my property, real and personal, even the shirt from my
back, shall be mortgaged to secure the payment of this marriage contract,
of the trousseau, and of the addition made to it, during my lifetime and
after my death, from the present day and forever."

_____, the bridegroom, has taken upon himself the responsi-
bility of this marriage contract, of the trousseau and the addition made to
it, according to the restrictive usages of all marriage contracts and the
additions to them made for the daughters of Israel, according to the insti-
tutions of our sages of blessed memory. It is not to be regarded as an inde-
cisive contractual obligation or as a mere formula of a document.

We have followed the legal formality of symbolic delivery (kinyan)
between _____ and of _____ this maiden and we have
used a garment legally fit for the purpose, to strengthen all that is stated
above,

AND EVERYTHING IS VALID AND CONFIRMED.

Witness _____   Witness _____

Interfaith Ketubot

Interfaith ketubot serve the same purpose as the new ketubot. They express, in writing, the love and commitment of the bride and groom. The only difference between the two documents is that the interfaith text either acknowledges the interfaith aspect of the couple's relationship, or it is written without mentioning any specific religion or faith.

Interfaith ketubot are not easy to find. Unlike standard ones, they are generally not displayed or advertised in Jewish bookstores or periodicals. In order to find what is available in your area, ask your rabbi or nearest Jewish bookstore or gift shop.

The following are three examples of interfaith texts.

Interfaith Ketubah #1

This ketubah witnesses before God, family, and friends that on the _____ day of the week, the _____ day of the month of _____ in the year 57_____ corresponding to the _____ day of the month of _____ in the year _____ here in _____, _____, the bride _____, and the groom _____, made this mutual covenant as equal partners in marriage.

With these rings we unite our hearts in tenderness and devotion. We will honor each other's culture as we link customs to form a trusting relationship. We will protect, support, and encourage each other as we create a loving future together. May our lives be intertwined forever and be as one in faith and in hope.

As we share life's everyday experiences, we promise to strive for an intimacy that will enable us to share our innermost thoughts and feelings; to be sensitive at all times to each other's needs; to share life's joys and to comfort each other through life's sorrows; to challenge each other to achieve intellectual and physical fulfillment as well as spiritual and emotional tranquillity.

We promise to establish a home for ourselves and our children shaped by our respective heritages; a loving environment dedicated to peace, hope, and respect for all people; a family filled with love and learning, goodness and generosity, compassion and integrity.

This marriage has been authorized by the civil authorities of the state of _____ and is in the spirit of the traditions of Moses and Israel.

Witness _____ Witness_____
Bride _____ Groom_____
Officiant _____ [1]

Interfaith Ketubah #2

מָצָאתִי אֶת שֶׁאָהֲבָה נָפְשִׁי

I Have Found The One In Whom My Soul Delights

On the _____ day of the week, the _____ day of _____ in the Jewish year 575_____, corresponding to the _____ day of _____, 199_____ of the Common Era, in the city of _____, _____, (the bride's name) and (the groom's name) entered into the covenant of marriage. They affirmed their love and commitment before a gathering of family and friends by exchanging rings and saying these words to each other: (or other words chosen by the couple)

I give you my hand and my love. I promise to share my life openly with you, to care for and comfort you, and to be your ally in good times and in troubled times from this day forward.

אֲנִי לְדוֹדִי וְדוֹדִי לִי.

I am my beloved's and my beloved is mine.

After having spoken the words and performed the rites which unite their lives, (the groom's name) and (the bride's name) became husband and wife, married in the eyes of God and according to the laws of the State of _____.

From every human being there rises a light that reaches straight to heaven. And when two souls are destined to find one another, their two streams of light flow together, and a single brighter light goes forth from their united being. (Baal Shem Tov)

יְבָרֶכְךָ יְיָ וְיִשְׁמְרֶךָ.

יָאֵר יְיָ פָּנָיו אֵלֶיךָ וִיחֻנֶּךָ.

יִשָּׂא יְיָ פָּנָיו אֵלֶיךָ וְיָשֵׂם לְךָ שָׁלוֹם.

May God bless you and keep you. May God's presence shine upon you and be gracious to you. May God's presence be with you and give you peace.

Bride _____ Groom_____
Witness _____ Witness_____
Rabbi _____[2]

Interfaith Ketubah #3

On the _____ day of the week, the _____ day of _____, _____, (bride's/partner's name), daughter/son of _____, and (groom's/partner's name), daughter/son of _____, say: This ring symbolizes our free decision to create this ceremony which joins us and is prompted by the love that we have for each other. This love provides us with the determination to be ourselves, the capacity to surrender and the push to live life to its fullest. It gives us the courage to hope and the ability to make our dreams a reality. Our purpose in joining together is to nurture that love in each other and, as best we can, give it to others.

We promise to try to be ever open to one another while cherishing each other's uniqueness, to comfort and challenge each other through life's sorrow and joy, to share our intuition and insight with one another, and above all to do everything within our power to permit each other to become the person we are yet to be.

We also pledge to establish a home open to the spiritual potential in all life. A home wherein the flow of the seasons and the passages of life are celebrated through the symbols of our heritages. A home filled with reverence for learning, loving, and generosity. A home wherein ancient melody, candles and wine sanctify the table. A home joined ever more closely to the communities of the world.[3]

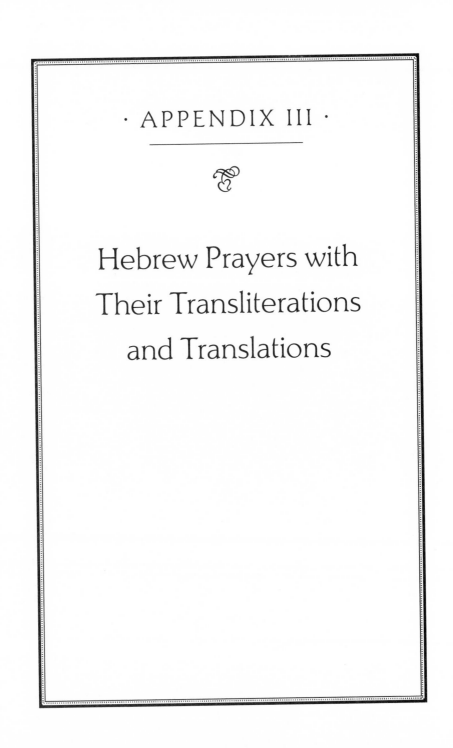

· APPENDIX III ·

Hebrew Prayers with
Their Transliterations
and Translations

This appendix includes the translations and transliterations of some of the most common Hebrew prayers and passages that are recited during an interfaith wedding ceremony. This section also includes the blessing over the bread, which is often recited at the reception, immediately before the meal is served.

Blessing over the Wine

בָּרוּךְ אַתָּה יְיָ אֱלֹהֵינוּ מֶלֶךְ הָעוֹלָם בּוֹרֵא פְּרִי הַגָּפֶן.

Ba-ruch a-tah A-do-nai, E-lo-hay-nu me-lech ha-o-lam, bo-ray p'ree ha-ga-fen.

Blessed are you, our God, Ruler of the Universe, Creator of the fruit of the vine.

Shehecheyanu

בָּרוּךְ אַתָּה יְיָ אֱלֹהֵינוּ מֶלֶךְ הָעוֹלָם שֶׁהֶחֱיָנוּ וְקִיְּמָנוּ וְהִגִּיעָנוּ לַזְּמַן הַזֶּה.

Ba-ruch a-tah A-do-nai, E-lo-hay-nu me-lech ha-o-lam, she-he-che-ya-nu v'kee-ye-ma-nu v'hee-gee-ah-nu laz-man ha-zeh.

Blessed are you, our God, Ruler of the Universe, who has given us life, sustained us, and permitted us to celebrate this joyous occasion.

Blessing over the Candle

בָּרוּךְ אַתָּה יְיָ בּוֹרֵא מְאוֹרֵי הָאֵשׁ שֶׁל הַשִּׂמְחָה שֶׁלָּנוּ.

Ba-ruch a-tah A-do-nai bo-ray m'o-ray ha-seem-cha she-la-nu.

Blessed are you, our God, who created the light of our celebration.

Exchange of Rings

Selection 1

Groom to the bride:

הֲרֵי אַתְּ מְקֻדֶּשֶׁת לִי בְּטַבַּעַת זוֹ כְּדַת מֹשֶׁה וְיִשְׂרָאֵל.

Ha-ray aht m'ku-de-shet lee, b'ta-ba-at zo, k'dat Mo-she v'yis-ra-el.

With this ring, be sanctified to me as my wife, according to the heritage of Moses and Israel.

Bride to the groom:

הֲרֵי אַתָּה מְקֻדָּשׁ לִי בְּטַבַּעַת זוֹ כְּדַת מֹשֶׁה וְיִשְׂרָאֵל.

Ha-ray a-ta m'ku-dash lee b'ta-ba-at zo k'dat Mo-she v'yis-ra-el.

With this ring, be sanctified to me as my husband, according to the heritage of Moses and Israel.

Selection 2

Groom to the bride:

הֲרֵי אַתְּ מְקֻדֶּשֶׁת לִי בְּטַבַּעַת זוֹ לְפִי הַמִּנְהָג.

Ha-ray aht m'ku-de-shet lee, b-ta-ba-at zo, l'fee ha-min-hag.

With this ring, be sanctified to me as my wife, according to ancient customs.

Bride to the groom:

הֲרֵי אַתָּה מְקֻדָּשׁ לִי בְּטַבַּעַת זוֹ לְפִי הַמִּנְהָג.

Ha-ray a-tah m'ku-dash lee, b'ta-ba-at zo, l'fee ha-min-hag.

With this ring, be sanctified to me as my husband, according to ancient customs.

Selection 3

Groom to the bride:

הֲרֵי אַתְּ מְקֻדֶּשֶׁת לִי בְּטַבַּעַת זוֹ לְפִי אֱמוּנָתֵינוּ.

Ha-ray aht m'ku-de-shet lee, b'ta-ba-at zo, l'fee e-mu-na-tay-nu.

With this ring, be sanctified to me, according to our beliefs.

Bride to the groom:

הֲרֵי אַתָּה מְקֻדָּשׁ לִי בְּטַבַּעַת זוֹ לְפִי אֱמוּנָתֵינוּ.

Ha-ray a-tah m'ku-dash lee, b'ta-ba-at zo, l'fee e-mu-na-tay-nu.

With this ring, be sanctified to me, according to our beliefs.

Selection 4

Groom to the bride:

הֲרֵי אַתְּ מְקֻדֶּשֶׁת לִי בְּטַבַּעַת זוֹ בְּעֵינֵי יְיָ.

Ha-ray at m'ku-de-shet lee, b'ta-ba-at zo, b'ay-nay A-do-nai.

With this ring, be sanctified to me, in the eyes of God.

Bride to the groom:

הֲרֵי אַתָּה מְקֻדָּשׁ לִי בְּטַבַּעַת זוֹ בְּעֵינֵי יְיָ.

Ha-ray a-tah m'ku-dash lee, b'ta-ba-at zo, b'ay-nay A-do-nai.

With this ring, be sanctified to me, in the eyes of God.

Selection 5

אֲנִי לְדוֹדִי וְדוֹדִי לִי.

Ah-nee l'do-dee v'do-dee lee.

I am my beloved's and my beloved is mine.

Selection 6

זֶה דוֹדִי וְזֶה רֵעִי.

Ze do-dee v'ze ray-ee.

This is my beloved and this is my friend.

The Seven Wedding Blessings

בָּרוּךְ אַתָּה יְיָ אֱלֹהֵינוּ מֶלֶךְ הָעוֹלָם בּוֹרֵא פְּרִי הַגָּפֶן.

Ba-ruch a-tah A-do-nai, E-lo-hay-nu me-lech ha-o-lam, bo-ray p'ree ha-ga-fen.

We praise you, Adonai our God, Ruler of the universe, Creator of the fruit of the vine.

בָּרוּךְ אַתָּה יְיָ אֱלֹהֵינוּ מֶלֶךְ הָעוֹלָם שֶׁהַכֹּל בָּרָא לִכְבוֹדוֹ.

Ba-ruch a-tah A-do-nai, E-lo-hay-nu me-lech ha-o-lam, she-ha-kol ba-ra lich-vo-do.

We praise you, Adonai our God, Ruler of the universe, who has created all things for your glory.

בָּרוּךְ אַתָּה יְיָ אֱלֹהֵינוּ מֶלֶךְ הָעוֹלָם יוֹצֵר הָאָדָם.

Ba-ruch a-tah A-do-nai, E-lo-hay-nu me-lech ha-o-lam, yo-tzer ha-a-dam.

We praise you, Adonai our God, Ruler of the universe, Creator of man and woman.

בָּרוּךְ אַתָּה יְיָ אֱלֹהֵינוּ מֶלֶךְ הָעוֹלָם אֲשֶׁר יָצַר אֶת-הָאָדָם בְּצַלְמוֹ בְּצֶלֶם דְּמוּת תַּבְנִיתוֹ וְהִתְקִין לוֹ מִמֶּנּוּ בִּנְיַן עֲדֵי עַד. בָּרוּךְ אַתָּה יְיָ יוֹצֵר הָאָדָם.

Ba-ruch a-tah A-do-nai, E-lo-hay-nu me-lech ha-o-lam, a-sher ya-tzar et ha-a-dam b'tzal-mo, b'tze-lem d'mut tav-nee-to, v'heet-keen lo mee-me-nu bin-yan a-day ahd ba-ruch a-tah A-do-nai yo-tzer ha-a-dam.

We praise you, Adonai our God, Ruler of the universe, who has fashioned us in your own image and has established marriage for the fulfillment and perpetuation of life in accordance with your holy purpose.

שׂושׂ תָּשִׂישׂ וְתָגֵל צִיּוֹן בְּקִבּוּץ בָּנֶיהָ לְתוֹכָהּ בְּשִׂמְחָה בָּרוּךְ
אַתָּה יְיָ מְשַׂמֵּחַ צִיּוֹן בְּבָנֶיהָ.

Sos ta-sees v'ta-gayl tzee-yon b'kee-butz ba-ne-ha l'to-cha
b'seem-cha, ba-ruch a-tah A-do-nai, m'sa-may-ach tzee-yon
b'va-ne-ha.

We praise you, Adonai our God, who blesses the joy of our
gathering. May rejoicing resound among your children everywhere through your love.

שַׂמֵּחַ תְּשַׂמַּח רֵעִים הָאֲהוּבִים כְּשַׂמֵּחֲךָ יְצִירְךָ בְּגַן עֵדֶן מִקֶּדֶם.
בָּרוּךְ אַתָּה יְיָ מְשַׂמֵּחַ חָתָן וְכַלָּה.

Sa-may-ach t'sa-mach ray-eem ha-a-hu-veem, k'sa-may-cha-
cha y'tzeer-cha b'gan e-den mee-ke-dem. Ba-ruch a-tah
A-do-nai, m'sa-may-ach cha-tan v'ka-la.

We praise you, Adonai our God, Ruler of the Universe,
source of all gladness and joy. Through your grace we attain
affection, companionship, and peace. Grant that the love
that unites this bridegroom and this bride may gladden
their souls.

בָּרוּךְ אַתָּה יְיָ אֱלֹהֵינוּ מֶלֶךְ הָעוֹלָם, אֲשֶׁר בָּרָא שָׂשׂוֹן
וְשִׂמְחָה, חָתָן וְכַלָּה, גִּילָה רִנָּה דִּיצָה וְחֶדְוָה, אַהֲבָה
וְאַחֲוָה, שָׁלוֹם וְרֵעוּת. מְהֵרָה יְיָ אֱלֹהֵינוּ יִשָּׁמַע בְּעָרֵי יְהוּדָה
וּבְחוּצוֹת יְרוּשָׁלַיִם, קוֹל שָׂשׂוֹן וְקוֹל שִׂמְחָה, קוֹל חָתָן וְקוֹל
כַּלָּה, קוֹל מִצְהֲלוֹת חֲתָנִים מֵחֻפָּתָם וּנְעָרִים מִמִּשְׁתֵּה
נְגִינָתָם. בָּרוּךְ אַתָּה יְיָ מְשַׂמֵּחַ חָתָן עִם-הַכַּלָּה.

Ba-ruch a-tah A-do-nai, E-lo-hay-nu me-lech ha-o-lam,
a-sher ba-ra sa-son v'seem-cha, cha-tan v'ka-la, gee-la ree-na
dee-tza v'ched-va, a-ha-va v'a-cha-va, sha-lom v'ray-ut.
M'hay-ra A-do-nai E-lo-hay-nu ye-sha-ma b'a-ray Ye-hu-da
uv-chu-tzot Y'ru-sha-la-yeem, kol sa-son, v'kol seem-cha, kol
cha-tan v'kol ka-la, kol metz-ha-lot cha-ta-neen may-chu-pa-

tam, u-ne-a-reem m'meesh-tay ne-gee-na-tam. Ba-ruch a-tah A-do-nai me-sa-may-ach cha-tan eem ha-ka-la.

We praise you, Adonai our God, ruler of the universe. Grant that there may be peace and tranquillity in their home, contentment and confidence in their hearts. We praise you, Adonai our God, who unites bridegroom and bride in holy joy.

The Priestly Blessing

יְבָרֶכְךָ יְיָ וְיִשְׁמְרֶךָ.

Y'va-re-che-cha A-do-nai v'yish-ma-re-cha.

May God bless you and keep you.

יָאֵר יְיָ פָּנָיו אֵלֶיךָ וִיחֻנֶּךָּ.

Ya-er A-do-nai pa-nav ay-le-cha vee-chu-ne-ka.

May God's countenance shine upon you and be gracious to you.

יִשָּׂא יְיָ פָּנָיו אֵלֶיךָ וְיָשֵׂם לְךָ שָׁלוֹם.

Yee-sa A-do-nai pa-nav ay-le-cha v'ya-sem le-cha sha-lom.

May God look upon you with favor and grant you peace.

Blessing over the Bread

בָּרוּךְ אַתָּה יְיָ אֱלֹהֵינוּ מֶלֶךְ הָעוֹלָם הַמּוֹצִיא לֶחֶם מִן הָאָרֶץ.

Ba-ruch a-tah A-do-nai, E-lo-hay-nu me-lech ha-o-lam, ha-mo-tzee le-chem min ha-a-retz.

Blessed are you, our God, Ruler of the universe, who brings forth bread from the earth.

Notes

Interfaith Wedding Ceremonies

1. Explanation by Marya De Carten, Episcopal priest.

Two Jewish-style Ceremonies

1. This is an interpretation, not a translation of the Hebrew, from *The Equivocal Wedding Service* by Samuel Glasner.
2. *Rabbi's Manual* (New York: The Central Conference of American Rabbis, 1961), p. 31.
3. This is an interpretation of the seven blessings by Rabbi Daniel Siegel.
4. This is an interpretation, not a translation of the Hebrew, from *The Equivocal Wedding Service* by Samuel Glasner.
5. Interpretation of the seven blessings by Linda Graetz and Jim Eng.
6. Ceremony created and provided courtesy of Linda and Jim Eng, married 1996.

Two Ceremonies Between a Catholic and a Jew

1. Translated by Stephen Tapscott © Pablo Neruda 1959 and Fundación Pablo Neruda, copyright © 1986 by the University of Texas Press.
2. Created and provided courtesy of Phil Samson and Martha Sperry, married 1995.
3. Ceremony created by and provided courtesy of Anita and Steve Georgon, married 1993.

Two Ceremonies Between a Protestant and a Jew

1. Adonai is one of many Hebrew words for God. Adonai is translated as "O Lord."
2. Ceremony created by and provided courtesy of Kim and Richard Lazarus, married 1995.
3. This is an interpretation, not translation, of the Hebrew blessing by Samuel Glasner from *The Equivocal Wedding Service*.
4. Music by Claude-Michel Schönberg; lyrics by Alan Boublil, Herbert Kretzmer, and Jean-Marc Natel.
5. These last two paragraphs are taken from Christian liturgy, including aspects of the Declaration of Consent/Intent.
6. This paragraph is taken from the Christian liturgy.
7. This paragraph is taken from the Jewish liturgy.
8. Ceremony created and provided courtesy of JoAnn and Steven Cooperstein, married 1992.

Opening Remarks and Blessings

1. This is an English interpretation, not translation, of the Hebrew, written by Samuel Glasner.
2. Created and provided courtesy of Diane and Bart Newland.
3. Adapted from "The Celebration and Blessing of Marriage," in *The Book of Common Prayer*.

Explanation of the Huppah

1. 15 Sivan 5742/June 6, 1982, for the *sheva b'rachot* of Yehuda Bodenstein Avniel and Sara Reva Horowitz, "The Succah and the Huppah" © 1982, Debra Cash.
2. Adapted from Anita Diamant, *The New Jewish Wedding* (New York: Simon & Schuster, 1985), pp. 91–92.
3. Excerpt from Debra Cash's poem, "The Succah and the Huppah."

Acknowledging Different Traditions

1. Created and provided courtesy of Phil Samson and Martha Sperry.

Acknowledging Children from a Previous Marriage

1. Created and provided courtesy of John Horst and Barbara Wallace.

Remembering Loved Ones Who Have Died

1. Written and provided courtesy of Beth Goldman, married 1997.

General Marriage Blessings and Prayers

1. It is a Jewish tradition to recite this prayer, called the Shehecheyanu, at joyous occasions.
2. Prayer from the *Rabbi's Manual* (New York: The Central Conference of American Rabbis, 1961), p. 29.
3. Adapted from *Rabbi's Manual*, p. 29.

Blessing over the Wine

1. *Rabbi's Manual* (New York: The Central Conference of American Rabbis, 1961), p. 31.
2. Ibid., p. 31.
3. Created and provided courtesy of Rabbi Wolli Kaetler.
4. Created and provided courtesy of George Schnee and Clara Silverstein.
5. Created and provided courtesy of Sara Rapport and Timothy Herbert.

Circling

1. Created and provided courtesy of Linda Graetz and Jim Eng.

Affirmation of the Families and of the Guests

1. *The Book of Common Worship*, p. 844.

Vows

1. Created and provided courtesy of Jim and Jennifer Glickman.
2. Created and provided courtesy of Jeffrey and Sharon Dodson.
3. Created and provided courtesy of Dana and Beth Ann Angelo.
4. Created and provided courtesy of Valerie Silverman and Michael Flaherty.
5. Adapted from the Catholic liturgy.

Ring Exchanges

1. *Rabbi's Manual* (New York: The Central Conference of American Rabbis, 1961), p. 30.

2. This is the traditional Jewish exchange of rings. It is not usually said in an interfaith ceremony because the phrase "in accordance with the traditions of Moses and Israel" implies that you are both Jewish. I included this exchange here because some rabbis do require both the Jewish and non-Jewish partner to say these words.

3. Adapted from *Rabbi's Manual* (New York: The Central Conference of American Rabbis, 1961), p. 30.

4. Created and provided courtesy of Louise Adler and Edward Liptak, married 1996.

5. Excerpt from the Catholic liturgy.

6. Excerpt from the Jewish liturgy.

The Unity Candle

1. Adapted from several different Christian sources.

2. From *The Book of Embraces* by Eduardo Galeano, translated by Cedric Belfrage with Mark Schafer. Copyright © 1989 by Eduardo Galeano. English translation copyright © 1991 by Cedric Belfrage. Reprinted by permission of the author and W. W. Norton & Company, Inc.

3. Created and provided courtesy of Phil Samson and Martha Sperry.

The Seven Jewish Wedding Blessings

1. Created and provided courtesy of Linda Graetz and Jim Eng.

2. Created and provided courtesy of Josh Roebuck and Louesa Schrim, married 1997.

3. "The Seven Wedding Blessings," from the *Rabbi's Manual* (New York: The Central Conference of American Rabbis, 1988), pp. 55–57.

4. Interpretation by Joan Kaye, in Anita Diamant, *The New Jewish Wedding* (New York: Summit Books, 1985), pp. 185–186.

5. Interpretation inspired by several different interpretations of the seven wedding blessings. Created and edited courtesy of Josh Roebuck and Louesa Schrim, married 1997.

6. Interpretation by Rabbi Daniel Siegel in Anita Diamant, *The New Jewish Wedding*, pp. 186–187.

7. Interpretation by David J. Cooper and Linda Hirschhorn, in Anita Diamant, *The New Jewish Wedding*, p. 188.

8. Adapted from the seven blessings written by David J. Cooper and Linda Hirschhorn, in Anita Diamant, *The New Jewish Wedding*, p. 188.

9. Blessing from the *Rabbi's Manual*, p. 31.

10. Seven contemporary blessings created and provided courtesy of Ron Shaich and Nancy Antonoacci, married 1998.

11. Yiddish word for pride and joy.

12. Created and provided courtesy of Irene Bell, the groom's grandmother.

13. Seven contemporary blessings, created and provided courtesy of Susan Gray and Adam Wisnia, married 1995.

14. Seven contemporary blessings created and provided courtesy by Linda Graetz and Jim Eng, married 1996.

15. Seven contemporary blessings created and provided courtesy of Susan Spector and Ed Brown, married 1997.

Closing Prayers and Readings

1. From a Unitarian wedding service in Abraham Klausner, *Weddings* (New York: Signet, 1986), p. 66.

2. Concluding prayer from the wedding ceremony in *The Book of Common Prayer*.

3. Adapted from various Catholic concluding prayers.

Breaking of the Glass

1. Created by and provided courtesy of Hope David and Robert Brown, married 1988.

Torah, or Hebrew Scripture, Passages

1. *Revised Standard Version* translation.
2. Jewish Publication Society translation.

Modern Poetry and Prose

1. Robert Creeley, *Collected Poems of Robert Creeley, 1945–1975* (Berkeley: University of California Press, 1983). Reprinted by permission of the University of California Press.

2. Robert Frost, *Complete Poems* (New York: Holt, Rinehart and Winston, 1969).

3. Translated by Stephen Tapscott © Pablo Neruda 1959 and Fundacion Pablo Neruda, copyright © 1986 by the University of Texas Press.

4. From *The Book of Embraces* by Eduardo Galeano, translated by Cedric Belfrage with Mark Schafer. Copyright © 1989 by Eduardo Galeano. English translation copyright © 1991 by Cedric Belfrage. Reprinted by permission of the author and W. W. Norton & Company, Inc.

5. "Desiderata" © 1927 by Max Ehrmann. All rights reserved. Reprinted by permission. Robert L. Bell.

6. From *The Prophet* by Kahlil Gibran. Copyright 1923 by Kahlil Gibran and renewed 1951 by Administrators CTA of Kahlil Gibran Estate and Mary G. Gibran. Reprinted by permission of Alfred A. Knopf, Inc. Also reprinted by permission of the Gibran National Committee, Beirut, Lebanon.

7. Ibid.

8. Translation copyright 1934, 1954 by W. W. Norton & Company, Inc., renewed © 1962, 1982 by M. D. Herter Norton. Reprinted by permission of W. W. Norton & Company, Inc.

9. Translation copyright 1934, 1954 by W. W. Norton & Company, Inc., renewed © 1962, 1982 by M. D. Herter Norton. Reprinted by permission of W. W. Norton & Company, Inc.

10. Excerpt from *The Little Prince* by Antoine de Saint-Exupery, copyright 1943 and renewed 1971 by Harcourt Brace & Company, reprinted by permission of the publisher. Also reprinted by permission of Heinemann Educational Publishers, a division of Reed Educational and Professional Publishing Ltd.

Appendix I: Traditional Wedding Ceremonies
A Reform Jewish Wedding

1. *Rabbi's Manual* (New York: Central Conference of American Rabbis, 1988), p. 51.

2. *Rabbi's Manual* (Philadelphia: Press of Maurice Jacobs, Inc., 1961), p. 31.

3. *Rabbi's Manual* (New York: Central Conference of American Rabbis, 1988), p. 55.

4. Ibid., p. 55–57.

5. Ibid., p. 58.

6. Ibid., p. 58.

A Roman Catholic Wedding

1. The English translation of the Rite for Celebrating Marriage between a Catholic and an Unbaptized Person from the *Rite of Marriage* © 1969, International Committee on English in the Liturgy, Inc. All rights reserved. Scripture excerpts are taken from the *Lectionary for Mass (New American Bible version)*. Copyright 1970 Confraternity of Christian Doctrine, Inc., Washington, D.C. Used with permission. All rights reserved. No part of the *Lectionary for Mass* may be reproduced by any means without permission in writing from the copyright owner.

An Episcopal Wedding

1. Episcopal service, *The Book of Common Prayer*, pp. 422–438.

A Presbyterian Wedding

1. Excerpts from the Theology and Worship Ministry Unit for the Presbyterian Church (USA) and the Cumberland Presbyterian Church, *Book of Common Worship* (Louisville, Ky.: Westminster/John Know, 1993), pp. 840–851.

Appendix II: Ketubot
Interfaith Ketubot

1. Ketubah text by Mickie and Eran Caspi, Caspi Cards and Art, Newtonville, Mass. Brochures of ketubah designs are available upon request. © 1991 Micha Klugman-Caspi. All rights reserved. May not be reprinted without permission.
2. Designed by Devon A. Lerner.
3. Ketubah written for Luana Silverberg-Willis and Yael Silverberg-Willis. Read to them by Rabbi Yoel Kahn. Text from Becky Butler, ed., *Ceremonies of the Heart* (Seattle: Seal Press, 1990), p. 69.